Advantium Publishing Company

Presents

FALLING AWAKE

Written By: L. Gartner
Copyright © 2025
All rights reserved.

Table of Contents

Evolutionary Gold (1)
Falling Awake (2)
The Hero's Journey (4)
The Trenches (5)
Life is but a Dream (6)
The Game of Life (7)
Biblical Santa Claus (9)
Mechanics of the Game (10)
The Golden Chalice (12)
Becoming Lucid (13)
Revealing What We Want (16)
Traveling the Spectrum (18)
Phases and Levels (20)
Discovering the Game (28)
The Heart of Perception (31)
Made You Forget (32)
Character = Story (35)
Dodging Beliefs (36)
Evolutionary Stalemate (39)
Comfortably Numb (40)
Gifts of our Lineages (41)
The Storyless Monk (42)
The Illusion of Time (44)
Programming Parameters (49)
Evolutionary Algorithms (51)
Pursuit of Happiness (53)
Versions of the Self (60)
Freedom is Choice (61)

Table of Contents

Family Money (64)
You: Version 2.0 (67)
Character Selection (69)
Crafting the Self (71)
Escaping Distraction (75)
Personal Power (78)
Upgrading the Loop (80)
Tuning In (81)
Setting Expectations (83)
The Hall of Golden Doors (85)
The Heart Unplugged (87)
Healing the Heart (89)
Emotional Dwellings (91)
Attractiveness (93)
Self-Connection (94)
Bridging the Gap (95)
External Feedback (99)
Shifting Your Reality (101)
The Inner Game (105)
Anchoring Points (106)
Bio-Reality (108)
True Reality (113)
Realm of The Ultimate (115)
Climbing the Mountain (119)
The Missing Piece (124)
You are the Star: The Hero (126)
The Edge of Reality (131)
Cerebral Clouds (132)
Virtual Life (133)
The Masters (136)

Evolutionary Gold

In the Game of Life our sole and primary purpose is to become the best version of ourselves. And as we progress along our personal path of evolution, we fulfill the age-old quests of the alchemists; transmuting lead into gold on this human journey of inner refinement as we evolve ourselves from water into the proverbial wine. Now we must admit that some people are a big murky glass of Mexico City tap water, others are a refreshing sip from a glacial spring, and a select few are a revelatory glass of vintage Chateau Margaux.

Attaining depth and awareness is a lifelong process, many lifetimes in fact and what I'm so fascinated by is why the hardest and most difficult experiences often hold the keys to the quantum leaps we make in our progress and evolution. A soufflé has got to bake in the oven for a while in order to reach its full potential and so too in every moment we are all subtly changing; sometimes for the better, sometimes not so much, and other times too busy fermenting in our own resistance to allow any real change to occur.

It's now abundantly clear to me that one does not become a fine wine without first squashing a few grapes. And in the Game of Life, each of those grapes just so happens to be a previous version of ourselves.

Falling Awake

It's sufficient to say that I've squashed the hell out of some of my previous versions. In fact, I received the inspiration for the cover of this book from a sign pinned to the wall directly across from a hospital bed I was strapped into. As I writhed in it with no recollection of how I got there or how I got the nasty concussion, two broken wrists and shattered foot I had been enduring for eighteen-hours without treatment, sleep or pain meds. Not to mention the added torment of having my broken wrists restrained; strapped to the sides of bed rails for having curtly demanded treatment. Now I wasn't belligerent or in a third world country so the only logical explanation for this and any other circumstance too ridiculous to be true was that I agreed to crank up the dial on the pressure cooker of life and bring myself within inches of my absolute threshold of pain and sanity, all in the name of waking myself up to the game.

As I waited in this bed in what seemed like eternal futility, hoping to begin the first of three surgeries to fuse plates into each of my wrists and screw my foot back together, I stared at this sign with such intensity that I'm truly astonished it did not burst into flames. I've heard it said that in times of torture or extreme pain, in a self-protective act the brain shuts off certain parts so that the pain's not felt anymore. I waited for this to happen— staring at this sign which was affixed crookedly so it appeared as though the figure was hopelessly free-falling into the seventh ring of hell.

This sign couldn't help but sear itself into my memory and following my recovery I set out to understand what it meant for me. This book is that assemblance of an answer, and the sign on its cover soon became the apt symbol of my awakening process. For me, life has been a visceral oscillation between sleepwalking through my existence and experiencing moments of profound clarity and inspiration. It's a continual process of trying to jostle my consciousness out of its acute state of narcolepsy and try as often as I can to remember to lift my head up out of autopilot and have a conscious look around.

Most of the time I'm a monk in my home, it's a sanctuary. I love the isolation, the space, the order and the calm. I thrive in this environment; it's my happy place. The moment I enter the outside world I feel like I shot-gunned a bottle of NyQuil as I stumble numb through a sea of overstimulation and crowds. My brain commandeers my body and everything becomes so lackluster, logical and automatic.

The only greater sanctuary than my home is being out in nature where I feel supremely connected, in the same way I imagine a Native American feels as they play a reed flute on a misty hillside.

Falling Awake is the perfect description to encapsulate my personal awakening process. And by awakening, I mean the continual moment-to-moment process of shaking one's self out of the cerebral slumber we slip into as we cruise control our way through a life half lived. Nourished only by the brief intermittent glimmers that come with fully experiencing something. For the last twelve years I've been diligently committed to my self-realization process, though very little of it has entailed me sitting stoically beneath a bodhi tree. It's clear I've chosen to set my game to the blood, sweat and tears mode of awakening, primarily because it's a much more interesting and accelerated version.

The Hero's Journey

Fundamentally we all love to tell a good story or at the very least live one, and that blood-sweat-and-tears is what makes for a great story. Nobody wants to hear about the times we've sipped margaritas on white sand beaches, but that time we dragged ourselves through enemy lines with a grenade in our teeth— everybody's all ears. Struggle, opposition, challenge and a passionate overarching goal is what makes the Hero's journey a compelling one.

In the process of learning how to write compelling stories I was immediately amazed by how much people love tension and how much it's an invaluably necessary part of driving the story and character forward. I also learned how universally the audience seems to feel that the good times are just fluff, meant only to serve as a temporary relief so we can take a collective breath and then watch the hero get back into the trenches so they can keep growing and inevitably achieve their goal. It's the hero's suffering that makes the triumph taste so sweet and without it it doesn't mean as much, in storytelling and in life. Understanding these modalities helped to transform my personal relationship with the story I was telling about my life and how I was relating to my own experiences.

Now I am not proposing that struggle is the only way to live an awakened life, but it's usually the most effective means of shaking us awake to realize what's not working and figure out how we're going to make things better. Once sufficiently aware of what's going on in and around us, we start to discover our power to craft our experiences instead of just making do with what comes our way. It's at this point that the game transforms and that default character living life in the trenches suddenly demonstrates a skill too valuable to waste with the slack-jawed sleepwalkers. And so they quickly rise the ranks of the game and if done effectively enough, they rise to a position that allows them to tip the scales and even change the game as we know it. Hero status.

The Trenches

For some reason many of us are under the false notion that struggle is noble, that it makes us a hard worker or a good person. Let me be the first to tell you that I'm not here to perpetuate this falsity. Struggling is far from noble, the noblest thing one can possibly do in life is thrive. Our primary purpose in life is to become the best version of ourselves and this process is greatly limited when all of our effort and energy is being used up just trying to survive. Our personal evolution is governed entirely by what we believe we are personally capable of doing, becoming, or experiencing in life. These beliefs are usually programmed by external feedback, through the way we were raised and how we see life play out for those around us. Then more often than not, we project a similar expectation onto our own experiences.

The trenches are designed for players to gain skill and experience through frequent challenges. If someone's teenager gets their driver's license they could take them for a few hours to practice driving around: Downtown, on a Friday, in rush hour, in the rain. And after their tremors subside, what they'll have is a much more experienced and capable driver. Time in the trenches is valuable because the trenches are specifically designed to make better players through voluminous challenge. If someone finds that they rarely ever have new experiences, try to avoid challenges, and have no interest in self-improvement, it's safe to say they're a mediocre player in the Game of Life; mediocre input with mediocre results, and a lot of people are completely fine with that.

Even if we're doing great in life, it's still just as easy to get comfortable and stagnate. Now on the other hand if someone consistently finds themselves in the trenches, it's only because they haven't yet developed the skill necessary to move up to a better level in the game. We can do that in a few ways: Intentionally learning the lessons our experiences are trying to teach us, becoming more aware of what's happening in and around us, resolving unconscious patterns of behaviour, and unembedding ourselves from our circumstance by choosing to engage with our experience from a state of observance rather than reactivity.

If something is just happening to us, then we are fully embedded in our experience of it and therefore have no power to guide or change it. Anything that triggers us into a reactionary state is our master until which point we're able to cultivate dominion over our reactions and emotional states. The moment we observe something we've disengaged from being embedded with it by creating the space of awareness between ourselves and what is happening. This buffer allows us the ability to actively guide its unfoldment and outcome, or at the very least consciously determine our relationship to it as we author this story we're telling about our experience and what it means for us.

Life is but a Dream

Still to this day I'm pretty sure that delirious hospital stay of mine was just a dream, and if it weren't for the scars I'd bet the farm on it. So what's the difference really, between waking reality and a dream? Both are planes for us to have experiences and as far as I'm concerned both of them are dream worlds; one is linear and the other is non-linear. We cannot take anything physical from one realm to the other and so we have no way of proving this world's realness in the other world and vice versa. When we are in the waking or dream world, that world is entirely real to us and forms our primary experience for as long as we're in it. We spend more time in the linear realm and because of its consecutive nature and buildability we ascribe it as the real one. At the end of the day, real is nothing more than a relative concept of sensual engagement. Both are real to us when we're in them, yet seemingly cease to exist when we are not. It would make sense that on a dual plane of reality this dream program of life we're in would be dual as well, in this case linear and non-linear.

Fundamentally the waking and dream realms are the same: planes of experience. And if we want to have any power to guide our experience in either realm, we must first become lucid; fully aware of what we are experiencing, then guiding our experience from that awareness for as long as we can until we're absorbed back into it.

The Game of Life

As we come into the remembrance that we are playing the most awesome game ever created and understand that we chose to upload our consciousness into this experience program of life on this planet. And that prior to doing so, we selected our avatar, our family, our core experiences, lessons and many of the other parameters that act as the framework of our game. All of which is uniquely designed to set the stage for our personal evolution so that we may become a lucid creator in the individual and collective dream that is Life. As with any game, we first must learn how to play and develop skill through experience so we may continually progress toward mastery.

In addition to choosing our own character we also cast the other characters in our game and the roles each of them will play, all of which is specifically designed to catalyze our personal growth either through support or opposition. The roles we assign others are generally archetypal and are all meant to elicit or reinforce certain aspects of our character and circumstance that are either supportive of our evolution or a necessary constraint designed to cause us to transcend a particular trait, belief, pattern or circumstance. If a character or experience has a large enough impact or constraint on us it can create the perfect environment for us to transcend to an entirely new level of being, which brings with it an entirely new version of reality.

Understanding the Game of Life is for obvious reasons the most important thing that one can do to become an exponentially better player. Now this is not some tiptoe-through-the-tulips, candy-land sort of game. It's not a toy, nor is it to be taken too lightly lest it bludgeon us to ashes. The purpose of the game, like most games, is incremental progression and as we move ever upward the sheer magic reveals itself to us on a much greater and grander scale.

So what exactly is the game?

The game is the most sophisticated, infinitely responsive experience program which we've entered to grow, evolve and benefit from having a human experience. The real power comes once we realize that we are in fact in the game and then initialize it as a conscious player. Like a dreamer who has become lucid and now has the power to affect the realm of their experience, so too are those who know they are in the game and play from a place of lucidity. Most players in the Game of Life are asleep in the sense that the game is playing them, in the same way a non-lucid dreamer is lead along by the dream they're having. They are embedded in what they are experiencing and so they have no power to guide or change it.

So how does one become lucid?

The first most basic purpose of the Game of Life is to realize that we're playing. The next task is to figure out the mechanics of how the game works and then practice what we know as we progress toward self-mastery. Becoming lucid in life is simply about being engaged with our experience in a manner that allows us to be fully in it but not of it, immersed in our experience but not embedded with it. It's paradoxical, but the only way to truly connect to our life is to separate ourselves from it through the space of our awareness.

Biblical Santa Claus

God, awesome and rather inconceivable, is not some biblical Santa Claus in the sky. It is the belief of the greatest masters throughout time that God is pure awareness, the purest, most supreme and infinite awareness there is. And we are on a journey which spans eons and carries us towards the evolutionary realization of this supreme level of awareness within ourselves. I never understood the treasure those half-naked yogis squatting in the caves of India had found until I came to this realization: God is pure awareness. And the higher level of awareness we embody determines the level of Creatorship we have in our lives. This is what is meant that we are Gods, crafted of the same thing from which we came: Awareness. And how aware we are on a daily basis, how directly we experience the happenings of our life as an extension of our own being is a direct measurement of the power we hold to shape our present and future experience, and possibly the future of all who will ever have a human experience.

This God level awareness is our true nature. It is the essence of who we are, like our own inner sun that is always shining behind the clouds of thought and the winds of human experience. Who we think we are is but a garment, a sheath placed over our true essence to have this temporary experience. Upon realizing this, our primary task then becomes to remove all of the obstructions, conceptions, distractions and compulsions which prevent our expression of this prime essence. This is the divinity we all contain; the spark of pure and eternal awareness which is the source of all creative power.

This God seed, like all seeds requires things to grow and those things are love and the light of our awareness, which are really one and the same. Now when I say love, I don't mean some hippy-dippy dancing in the fields with flowers in our hair kind of love. Love is the highest form of existence. If God is the purest most infinitely encompassing awareness, Love is its first expression; the prime emanation and highest form of existence, a supreme beingness both tender and nourishing. We live eternally coddled within this loving awareness but most of the time we're too busy mindlessly dragging ourselves through life to realize the magnitude of what is really at hand here.

The purpose of life is to reveal who we truly are as we move toward becoming an emanation of this supreme awareness. That is the goal of the game. It's the prize hidden in the tallest tower of the castle high up on the hill, its light beckoning to us as we stand in the muddy field thick with bristles and thornbrush. Yet paradoxically it is also the thing we've had all along. Understanding the goal of the game gives us a great deal of context so that we may then move on to understanding the mechanics of how it works.

Mechanics of the Game

The first key to claiming our power as a creator being in the Game of Life is accepting responsibility for everything that has or will happen. A lot of people are unwilling to do that and so they remain asleep to their creative power. If things are just happening to us then we are but a pawn on the chessboard of life, insignificant and often used as a necessary sacrifice. The truth is we choose everything prior to and during the entirety of our experience. The game is a completely customized interface of experience which is programmed with our parameters; core experiences, lessons, characters and revelations that will move us forward in our journey of self-realization and Creatorship.

The game is built upon the principles of polarity. Like a chessboard of both light and dark squares and pieces, it is there as a means of creating harmony and balance as both expressions play an invaluable role in the evolutionary process. Most people think of polarity in terms of good and bad, but that is a very limited way of perceiving it. In its most fundamental form polarity is positive and negative and its expression is either expansive or constrictive.

Everything within the game is specifically designed to either expand us, or act as a necessary constraint as we prepare ourselves for expansion. There's a reason why the greatest artists, writers, leaders etc., had a hell of a time getting there, because the more we wade through constrictive forces the more brilliant and multifaceted a diamond we are forged into. We are all well aware of our personal capacity for pain and suffering and design things accordingly prior to coming in, though at times we do push ourselves to the very threshold of our limits in the name of growth and expansion. It's true that the game can be incredibly challenging but that's what makes it a great game with great rewards.

Most of us have this false notion that if we just get rich then the game won't ever be hard again. The game is supposed to be challenging and that's meant to be a big part of the fun. Who wants to play go-fish their whole life? I mean some people do but that's not for me, and if you've gotten this far it's probably not for you either. The game is meant to be challenging, the whole point of the game is to become a good enough player where every challenge is seen as an opportunity to showcase our skills. That's the fundamental framework of every game.

The Golden Chalice

A pivotal part of becoming a truly great player in the Game of Life is integrating the ego, most people say we have to shed it but what we have to do is transmute and integrate it. Remember, we are on the alchemist's journey of turning lead into gold and in this case it's turning the lead of unawareness into the gold of supreme lucidity.

We may look upon the ego as a golden chalice in the Game of Life, which is definitely a symbol the ego would choose to represent itself. The ego is a crystallization of our individual will and desire and it is comprised of all the *things* we think will make us who we want to be. The game loves paradoxes and so the ego is the golden chalice we wander the external world holding in our hand looking for things to fill it with, but the more we do the more we come to realize that it's bottomless. How we transmute the golden chalice of the ego is to reintegrate it into our inner world and fill it from within.

The ego appears to us as the great treasure of the golden chalice, yet aside from its illusory yet dazzling appearance it's nothing more than a hungry-hungry-hippo gobbling up all it can in an attempt to fill the void and feel satisfied. And the more we try to fill it with the things of the external world the emptier it grows. This is purposefully designed to turn us within once we realize the external world does not hold the treasures we are actually seeking. In the outer world the chalice is a negative instrument, meaning it's subtractive and everything we fill it with only increases its need for more which is what makes it bottomless. When the chalice is integrated within it becomes a positive instrument, meaning it's additive and everything put into it is only added upon and so our cup runneth over.

Simply put it's where the anchor of our self-worth is set, in the external world or the internal world. When anchored in the external the chalice is built to serve one's ego, when anchored within the chalice is built to serve one's being. It's always clear to differentiate those who have or are in the process of achieving this great work.

Recently I heard a parable that when God was looking for a good place to hide divinity he decided to hide it inside of us because it would be the last place anyone would look. And in many people, His secret is still safe.

Once we quit striving to make ourselves more impressive externally, we start to unembed ourselves from the demo-mode of the game and our liberation process begins. We can still achieve great things but it's no longer being done as a means to prove our worth or greatness. Many of us discover that when we do start to awaken, we often find ourselves mid-stride, living a life that's not what we want. And so there's this limbo phase of awakening, when we're lucid enough to know we're dreaming but not lucid enough to create our experience and it's this phase where we need to learn how things work, which is the purpose of this book.

Becoming Lucid

The Game of Life is dual in nature and so there are two modes of expression and experience: Illusion and Awareness. The negative mode of experience is one of Constrictive Illusion while the positive mode of experience is of Expanded Awareness and we travel this spectrum between illusion and awareness all day long, every day of our lives.

In the Game of Life there are things that we must wake up from, things that put us and keep us asleep. These things anchor us into Constrictive Illusion, which it's important to note is only sustained by the energy we feed it. The reality of Constrictive Illusion operates on a specific electromagnetic bandwidth which govern the emotional states of worry, fear, resistance, anger, boredom, judgement, superiority, escapism, loneliness, frustration and disappointment. Anytime we're experiencing any of these states it's safe to say that we're asleep and the game is playing us.

There are also many things that wake us up and help us to anchor into the reality of Expanded Awareness which operates on the electromagnetic bandwidth of contentment, love, peace, gratitude, connection, beingness, satisfaction and synchronicity. If we're experiencing any of these states, it's safe to say we're in a state of awareness and lucidity. One can evoke these states through conscious breathing, mindfulness, new experience, excitement, kindness, connection, going for a walk, being in nature, learning, sharing, expanding beyond one's comfort zone, introspection and meditation. The key is to find which ones work most effectively for us and to implement them often.

Becoming lucid in life is a moment-to-moment process and the first key is becoming aware of when we're asleep and knowing how to wake ourselves up. We all have triggers, and we'd be wise to know exactly what they are. Understanding the positive and negative states we're prone to experiencing allows us to develop ways to pull ourselves into or out of them.

If the point of the game is to become an expression of supreme creative awareness, then naturally much of the game will be designed to wake us up in whatever ways we respond to most. Then as we increase our lucidity, we'll encounter our triggers to see how well we're anchored into our awareness. At first they'll be small things which will likely increase to comprehensively test our balance.

It's important for us to note that once we reach a certain level of lucidity we will be rigorously tested with past triggers and emotional debris. The main reason for this is that there are pivotal points in the Game of Life when we're coming into a significant amount of creative power and just as we wouldn't give our narcoleptic teenager the keys to the car, so too are we recovering from narcolepsy as we move towards a more wakeful and lucid existence. In the meanwhile as we build our lucidity we move along a sort of graduated licensing system as we demonstrate that we can drive our experience without incident; proving we have the awareness needed to use our creative power well, in a way that serves us and those around us.

If at any point we feel like life is just senselessly pummelling us it's because it's trying valiantly to shake us awake to recognize a lesson, unresolved issue or pattern. And if we greet our experience with awareness things will improve almost immediately, especially if we ask what we could learn about our fears or beliefs based on the challenge we're facing. Then, examine any repeating patterns and get to the root of the feeling they're reinforcing, tracing the root of that feeling back to when we first felt that way so we may acknowledge its source and process it.

Every single one of us is a creator of our life, it's just that most of us are doing it in unconscious and unserving ways. When we are not well anchored into our awareness the external world becomes a hopelessly intricate distraction from coming more fully into our power. Unanchored we are like a tiny rowboat on a rising sea with spoons for oars. On the other hand, when we are well anchored into the center of our awareness we become one with the eye of the storm and the experiences of the world dance around us in all their wonder and magnificence.

Revealing What We Want

Prior to entering the Game of Life each of us chose some very important parameters of our game. One important aspect we chose are the themes we've come to realize in this lifetime; this can be things like freedom, compassion, self-empowerment, true love or self-realization, the list is endless. The game is built as an expression of polarity which means that we're generally set on a path that is often filled with polarizing experiences that have us feel and encounter the opposite of what we're seeking so that we may incrementally progress along the spectrum towards its realization and tasting so much sweeter having known its opposite.

In India there's a Sanskrit phrase called Netti-Netti which means "not this, not that." We essentially three-little-bears our way through life, experiencing too hot and too cold until we know what just right means to us. Polarization allows us to discover our own ideals because happiness is entirely relative. What one person considers to be heavenly could feel like a packed city bus to someone else. So we often have to wade through what we don't want in order to figure out what exactly we do. It's just that a lot of people choose from what they don't want because they thought those were the only options and so they settled. Life is a catalogue and the more we engage with it as such, the more it responds to us in that manner.

Anytime we're actively seeking something: a place to live, a job, a car, a vacation destination, a mate, anything really, the field of our experience responds to our intention and provides us with options within the range of limits and standards we've set. Each option that presents itself gives us the ability to intelligently guide the process. By understanding what exactly we like or don't like about what is being presented we begin to reveal what we're actually looking for, because only then will we have the opportunity to find it. Most people have a vague and distant mirage of what they desire and so they languish with no clear direction toward realizing it.

Standards play a huge role in all of this because we determine the quality we receive based on our choices and our choices are influenced by the depth of our understanding of what exactly we're looking for. The key is to have a very clear understanding of what we want and the discipline not to settle until we find it. Happiness is entirely relative so the game assumes that we know what we're doing and that we're choosing the things we want, because why would we choose anything else? Whatever we're giving our awareness to we are proclaiming loudly for the game to give us more of it. The greatest resource we have in life is our focus and the things we pay attention to will grow and eventually reap dividends so it's important to invest wisely.

The game is built to keep us engaged, so if something is capturing our attention and engaging us, we will be sent more of it. It's actually a very beneficial arrangement, it's just the primitive aspects of our brains tend to make a mess of things; obsessing over what we don't want or that we don't have what we do want.

Once we start bringing awareness to our choices and experiences the game transforms because it's designed to present to us things that are aligned with what we're choosing through our thoughts, feelings, speech and actions. So when we choose things from a higher level of awareness, higher level things are presented to us in return. Just as a social media stream suggests to us content based on what we're giving our attention and engagement to, so too does reality. Once we realize this and consciously engage with the process it will completely transform.

Remember, the Game of Life isn't supposed to be too easy, a game that's too easy isn't fun but neither is playing a game we're not good at. So since this is the game we've signed up for it would benefit us greatly to learn how to play it and play it well. A great game isn't easy, it's that the challenges are fun because we're refining our skill set and rising to the occasion. And those who choose to be serious students of the game are the masters in the making who will likely shape the game as we know it.

Traveling the Spectrum

Up until now we have discussed the Game of Life as an abstract thing, but the experience program that forms what we know as our reality contains within it a framework of incremental levels. Each level has ten sub-levels. Imagine a spectrum from 1-10, which are the sublevels we are traversing on whatever our current level is, as we move towards the next phase of our game and development.

Once we reach apex (the peak point of our current level) if we did not successfully complete the tasks and reach the level of lucidity required to unlock the next level, we must try that level again until we succeed. Often when we don't pass into the next phase or level but are doing well in our progress, we are rewarded for our effort with an apex experience; this could be a burst of inspiration, a deep revelation, a glimpsing of a higher state of being, or just having an amazing time with friends. It all depends on the individual and where they are on their path.

After our cosmic pat on the head, we're then bounced back to base (the beginning point of our current level) so that we may face the weak points in our game, patch up the leaks and tighten up our skills in hopes that we may perform well enough this round to graduate to the next phase or level. It's important to understand that this process is just as much of an internal journey of transcendence as it is an external one, and as we come to realize greater levels of understanding and awareness within ourselves, greater levels will also reveal themselves in the world of our experience.

Now imagine we're in a speed boat, motoring across the spectrum from 1 to 10 and the wake of the boat is causing debris in the water to float to the surface. In the same way, the energetic wake we create as we ascend the levels kicks-up all of the triggers, emotional debris and collective constructs we're still wrestling with. Then when we are sent back to base, reworking our way through the sub-level spectrum 1 to 10 we will encounter these things on our path so that they may be processed and resolved, because each of them is a limit to us and is siphoning our power and energy.

It's amazing how much we feed the things that do not serve us, so a huge part of leveling up is realizing what they are, why they have a hold on us, and then releasing them as effectively as possible. This is simply done through self-awareness and introspection because the moment we become aware of something it is no longer being programmed into our experience unconsciously. Once we're aware of a narrative, behavior, pattern or trigger we then have the choice to respond differently and redefine our relationship to it, and in doing so not feed it any of our energy the next time it arises.

On the other hand if someone is not encountering many triggers or challenges one of two things is likely true; they either excessively use means of escapism or distraction and don't face what is trying to greet them on their path, or they are moving so slowly across the sublevels that there isn't enough momentum to create an energetic wake to stir things up and so stagnation sets in.

This means that if we're encountering triggers and challenges it's a good thing, counterintuitive I know, but it's because each challenge is an opportunity to tighten up our game and make a quantum leap in our skill level. The more awareness we bring to our experience the easier, more enjoyable and exponentially progressive our journey will be. This perspective takes practice but so does doing anything well.

Phases and Levels

The Game of Life contains within it five phases and thirty-three primary levels. We may better understand our progression through these levels if we look upon the framework of the game as operating as a graduated licensing system, incrementally progressing us towards full remembrance and lucidity so that we may claim the creative power that comes with it.

The 5 Phases of The Game of Life

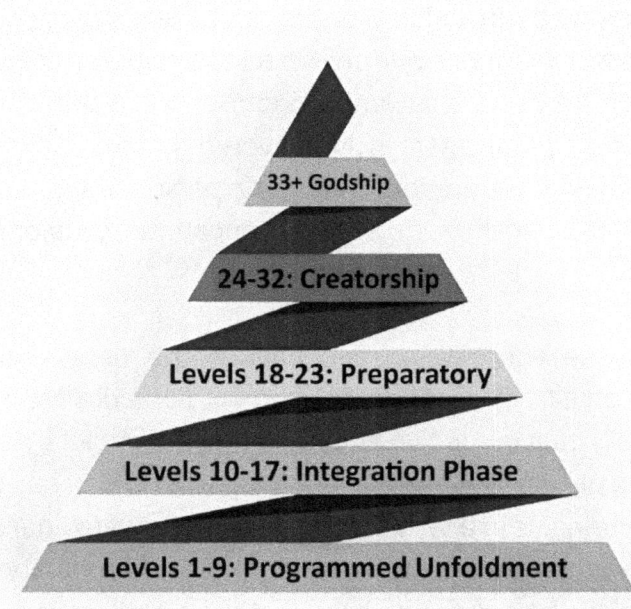

Phase 1: Levels 1-9, Programmed Unfoldment
Phase 2: Levels 10-17, The Integration Phase
Phase 3: Levels 18-23, The Preparatory Phase
Phase 4: Levels 24-32, The Creatorship Levels
Phase 5: Levels 33+, The Godship Levels

Phase 1: Levels 1-9, Programmed Unfoldment

The first phase of levels is the demo-mode of the game where the program is running with little to no input from the player, like a non-lucid dreamer who's just along for the ride. The primary purpose of this phase is to experience our pre-selected programming, which is comprised entirely of the parameters chosen by us prior to initializing the game. These parameters include everything that makes up the conception of who we are: our backstory, personality traits, core experiences, relationships, polarization encounters, major life lessons, etc.

This is the phase where we are seemingly at the mercy of our experience, on a track of predestination with practically no choice or control. This is because we've already made the choices we're now experiencing prior to initializing the game, all of which has been designed to bring us in a very specific manner towards our self-realization and development. A large majority of humanity has remained in this first phase of levels lifetime after lifetime, though many of us are now ascending into the higher levels.

The focus of the first phase is purely to experience all of the things we've programmed in, all of which is meant to craft the character we are in the process of becoming: The Hero of The Game. Every aspect of our programming is also meant to create a very specific void which we'll eventually get to fulfill once we reach the higher levels. The difficulty level we set in this initial phase is reflective of our skill level and the ability we have to ascend. It also directly determines the amount of rewards, level of power, and sphere of influence that will eventually be made available to us as a result. In other words, the more challenging our programming, the greater the risk of us staying asleep but also the greater the rewards we receive upon waking up.

Simply put, the bigger the dreams we have, the deeper we're going to sleep and the more blood, sweat and tears it's going to take to wake us up.

Transcending into the next phase of levels requires a substantial amount of introspection and a conscious processing of the past in order to unhook from our autopiloted programming. As we start to understand that everything that has or will happen is meant to serve us in our awakening process, we begin our required departure from a victim mentality and move toward anchoring into the understanding and awareness necessary to move on to the next phase of levels. Only once we have perspective and understanding can we create the space necessary to loosen the embedded control our programming is deliberately designed to have on us.

It is very important to note that our pre-selected programming is only meant for the first phase of the game and no others. It is specifically designed to imbue us with the qualities, experiences and realizations necessary in order to successfully travel the path we designed to wake us up through suffering, soul searching and persistent experiences of the opposite of what we truly desire to be or have. We must recognize the programming of our past for what it is if we are to transcend it. This requires a willingness to bring awareness to it as a whole, as well as to any specific instances of unresolved trauma which are the most deeply embedded aspects of the programming we selected.

We must attain awareness and integration of our programmed phase and the greatest aid in doing this is understanding that each challenge and difficulty is meticulously designed to carry us forward in some way. For any unresolved issues, it's important for us to connect with the way that experience made us feel and understand the beliefs we formed as a result of feeling that way. Lastly, we must consciously assert what we know to be true about ourselves and our lives, now, at our current level of awareness.

This phase of our character development is built entirely upon the things that have or will happen to us. This is by intelligent design because for as long as we're unaware that we are playing, the game needs to find ways to teach us how to play, evolve and hopefully—wake up. This usually starts by eliciting experiences that make us feel certain ways, believe certain things, and help us to integrate the experiences and attributes needed to evolve our character.

Much of what is brought forth in this phase are circumstances that help to bring to our attention the things that are keeping us from realizing our potential so that we may come to realize a greater version of ourselves and our life.

Every difficulty we program into our experience is meant to be a means of awakening and transcendence. In the first phase, challenges are there purely to develop us into the character we chose to become in this game. In the phases to follow, any challenges we encounter are there to point out a specific weak point in our game, or rather an area in which an issue remains that is preventing us from fully claiming our creative power. The Game of Life is above all a learning program and the more we actively engage in our experience as a student of it, the faster we graduate the levels.

Phase 2: Levels 10-17, The Integration Phase

In this phase of levels the autopiloted mechanism recedes in proportion to the amount the individual has loosened and shed their programming. The primary realization of this phase is that our programmed experiences *do not* determine who we are, that we have the power to determine who we are and that in turn determines the relationship we have to our experiences. And so we shift from being imprinted by our experience to imprinting on it.

We also discover an increased ability to choose and guide our experience. There are still some core experiences and contracted dynamics programmed in but we now have the opportunity to experiment with our power of choice, though the scope of options and experiences available to us is still limited in order to keep us within wandering distance of the path we're on. We continue to expand our understanding of the role we play in our life as we experiment with the creative power we have to guide it, which expands as we cultivate our inner world and make choices from an increasingly higher perspective and understanding.

Phase 3: Levels 18-23, The Preparatory Phase

In this phase of levels we are crossing the threshold of polarization, meaning we no longer have to experience the opposite of what we desire in order to discover what our desires are. We have a clear understanding of who we are and what we want and are able to create beneficial circumstances and relationships to support us in our process of becoming. This phase can at times have a distinct feeling of purgatory, like a cosmic holding room where there are no substantial anchors to the past and yet none of the big things we desire are showing signs of developing in the future.

There will be distinctive bouts of feeling like we're just spinning our wheels. Both the previous and current phase prompt a natural shedding of programmed memories, so it's common for individuals to find themselves with very few recollections of the past because of the continual relinquishing of programming.

As we near completion of this phase of levels it's important to note that we will be rigorously triggered and tested to ensure that we are not bringing any trauma algorithms or negative patterning into the next phase of the Creatorship levels. It is at this point in the phase where many on the path can feel disheartened by the fact that they had come so far yet find themselves back dealing with the same old emotional debris, but this is only because that debris can and will not pass through the etheric membrane separating this phase with the next one.

This elongated membrane acts as the megalithic bridge into the Creatorship levels. It is a great chasm which only those whom through rigorous testing have proven themselves to be truly clear and capable shall pass into Remembership and enter victorious into the Creatorship levels, having successfully completed the biggest and most momentous leap in The Game of Life.

Phase 4: Levels 24-32, The Creatorship Levels

Cue the trumpets. The focus of this phase of levels is to support us in coming more fully into our creative power as we build our life to be as we will it to be. Many auspicious happenings, lucky breaks and chance connections unfold to aid us in realizing a much higher version of our self, our life and the contribution we will make to the collective. It is in this phase of levels where we may fully realize what an ideal life means to us and then build out our vision.

This phase is the fabled somewhere over the rainbow where dreams come true. As the veils of the previous levels continue to fall away, what more fully reveals itself is the realization that we are center of our universe and everyone and everything is a reflection of who we are and what we're emanating. We understand intrinsically that every moment is specifically designed for our fulfillment as well as to aid us in our growth and development, as we anchor into full lucidity within our dream life.

Now it's important to note that this does not mean that we will never again encounter any challenges, challenge is a necessary part of the growth and refinement process. No challenge, no growth. But the key difference is that now we've developed enough awareness that we're not absorbed by the challenges we encounter and so we retain the fullness of our power to guide the unfoldment of things towards our benefit. In order to pass into the next phase and into the Godship levels a great deal of self-mastery and altruistic creatorship must be demonstrated.

Phase 5: Levels 33+
The Godship Levels

Cue the choir of angels. The clouds part and golden rays rest upon our head. The focus of this phase of levels is to expand one's creative power to encompass collective reality and the world at large, meaning that as we demonstrate a masterful level of understanding and sufficiently exemplify correct use of our creative power, we incrementally expand our sphere of influence. This often raises one to a role where they are benevolently shaping and guiding collective reality in their own unique way.

Whether we believe Jesus to be a historical or allegorical figure; he was 33, or rather he was operating within the Godship levels, as this number is much more indicative of a level of lucidity and Creatorship than a calendar age. Every ascended master who has successfully entered the Godship levels has access to what the ordinary levels would consider miraculous, simply because the laws that govern the higher levels transcend the conception of what the lower levels know to be possible. This is because each time we ascend to a higher phase of levels we shed some of the frameworks built in to safely girder our power and potential. Essentially the training wheels come off because we're continually demonstrating our ability to masterfully utilize our power with great benefit to ourselves and others. It is in this phase where one may truly come to know the magic of creation and fully realize ourselves as the conduits for it.

Tearing the Veil

Fifteen years ago a flower-child friend of mine brought me to an ayahuasca ceremony in California. Clearly miracles do happen because there I was about to dive face first down a sage scented rabbit hole. She picked me up at my place and we drove up through Topanga Canyon together.

Both nervous and excited, I had no idea what to expect. She had referenced "they" throughout our conversation, telling me that "they" have a great sense of humor and that she thinks "they" are going to share a lot of important things with me tonight. I assumed she meant her fellow hippie hipsters; she did not. She meant more of a proverbial *They*. I like to think of them as ground control on the other side of the game, behind the veil. They are the ones who've beaten the game and help others get better at it too. Much of what I experienced transcends language, but I'll make do. For me this ceremony was the equivalent of that tunnel you go down in Super Mario Bros into a room full of coins: Ching-ching-ching. I was collecting treasure, and it was all in the form of accessing a level of awareness I've never glimpsed before. This moment put an irreparable tear in the veil of my narcolepsy which was the opening that grew and still continues to till this day. I've done a couple of ceremonies in the years since then and have made some observations I will now share:

Each ceremony has three distinct waves of energy. The first is a wave of Divine Masculine energy, the second is a wave of Divine Feminine energy and then comes the wave of The Ultimate. These three waves cycle in three times throughout the duration of the ceremony, each time bringing in a higher octave of energy. In essence these ceremonies are energetic activations and sometimes they can be turbulent while at other times it's smooth sailing, it all depends on the emotional debris we're carrying into the process with us.

When I reach the summit of the energies and sit upon the peak of the experience, I'm not high at all. I feel clear and sit in the pure isness of the moment. "It just is" I observe mentally to myself. There's this paradoxical feeling of remembering and forgetting at the exact same time. My mind was not really able to produce anything other than the observation that it just is.

Part of me noticed that I wasn't satisfied by the isness of it. The monkey brained mouth-breather in me was like: "This is it? Isness—Where's the bliss? The ecstasy. What kind of prize is that?" But over the years as I grew up, or in rather, I realized that everything lies in that isness, it comprises the very fabric of our reality and holds within it our very existence. It contains all power, potential and magic which is revealed to those who have the eyes of awareness to see it.

To those who ask me if I'd suggest doing an ayahuasca ceremony my response is only to do it if they're willing to wade neck deep in the sticky mud of their own unconscious. Because even if one has a transcendently beautiful experience, the energetic activations behind these ceremonies press the go button on our evolution, and some would prefer to take the easy road and remain the same in a perpetual state of tolerable stagnancy.

Evolution is messy and uncomfortable but the fruit it bears is well worth the toiling, though it's not for the faint of heart. It's true that we're all on a path of evolution but some rise to the occasion more willingly than others because it takes a warrior's spirit to drag ourselves through the rough patches. In the long run, evolving is a lot easier than living an unfulfilling life; falling asleep alone to whatever is on Netflix with a plate of dismantled chicken wings on my chest.

>   I'll choose the mud thank you.

I do feel that these ceremonial experiences have allowed me to be in the immaculate presence of the Divine, the one who has many names and rendered me wholly reverent with such a profoundly deep sense of respect that I'd never before experienced. These experiences changed me, but the fascinating thing is we often forget all about it once we come back down from the ceremonial level. These higher levels always remain available for us to access naturally but it requires shedding a great deal of the mental constructs and perceptive filters we carry with us through everyday life.

The Heart of Perception

The brain looks at the magic of existence and dismantles it into ordinary lackluster pieces. It is only through direct experience that we can restore the magic inherent in life, but this can only be done through the heart rather than the mind. The mind looks at a bird and sees a thing with feathers that produces sound. The heart looks at a bird and is moved by it. A child inherently lives from the heart and so too must we return to a state of openhearted awareness if we wish to connect with the higher realms of experience available to us in every moment.

Doing so requires us to get out of our head, out of our comfort zone, out of our routine, and put ourselves out there to experience and explore. This is how we grow and connect more fully to ourselves and our experience. Many of us feel disconnected from ourselves and others and above is listed the recipe to resolve that should anyone wish to.

Enlightenment is not this fabled distant thing; it's the process that is currently underway in every one of us as we more fully embody the light of our awareness and move toward increasing our level of wakefulness and lucidity. True awareness is centered in the heart, so if we wish to become more lucid then transcending the mind is a big part of the process and that begins with becoming aware of our thoughts and cultivating them through mindfulness and observation. Those who are able to transcend their mind can connect with an intelligence infinitely greater than any human mind, and it is from this universal intelligence where all great things arise.

What's becoming increasingly more apparent is that psychedelics may be helpful for some in their evolutionary journey, but it's certainly not required as there are completely natural ways to access these higher transcendent states. Some say fasting or exertion breeds higher states, others mantra meditations. For me personally I've seen that holotropic breathwork has led me to the same ceremonial level of experience and energetic activation. Ecstatic dance and cold plunges also have the potential to lead to transcendent states but it requires a great deal of surrender in order for transcendence to be achieved.

Made You Forget

The fundamental impediment of the game is that it can get us to forget who we are, and at times it can hurdle every possible circumstance that has us believe that we are not who we thought we were. Life can both lull and pummel us into forgetting and in this forgetfulness we go on living a life that is not really ours, as we play a much lesser character in a story that doesn't really belong to us. One of the greatest errors we make as players is letting the game define the character we are playing; meaning allowing what happens to shape our conception of ourselves and the life we're living. Only once we no longer allow the story to define us are we free to start defining the story.

The people who achieve great things in life do so because they flip the script, no longer is their character defined by the story the game is telling. They know who they are and what they came to do and regardless of what they experience it's not going to change that. There are so many examples of people who persisted in who they are and what they came to do and as a result shaped history and the world as we know it. It took Thomas Edison 1,000 attempts to make the incandescent light bulb. Before attaining global legend status Marilyn Monroe was fired from Columbia Pictures because they believed she lacked any star quality. Walt Disney was turned down

302 times for the loan he needed to build Disneyland. The people who allow themselves to be defined by their circumstance are the ones who shrink back from failure and in doing so they forfeit the game. Those who press on do so because they know that failure is often just a necessary part of the process, just a rung on the ladder they are climbing up to reach their goal.

The density of our initial programming is what gets us to fall asleep and believe in a false story by externally reinforcing it through our experiences. And we willfully sign up for this knowing that we're good enough players to wake up and remember who we are and by extension the life we came to live, then impose our will through unwavering insistence until our external world yields to us.

Once we tell our own story and take the story out of what is happening on the surface of our experience, eventually it conforms to our will. If we are not intentionally telling the story, the story is telling us. The story is where the power is. Many people allow their circumstance to have the power over them because it's the one leading the narrative. Once we understand that all experience is fundamentally neutral and that we assign all meaning to our experience, we discover our power to take back the wheel and start directing it to take us where we want to go.

The premise of the game we are playing is simply to remember who we are in our highest expression. The initial phase of the game is designed to have us believe that we're something we're not; that we are the illusion of our circumstance. This is an integral part of our awakening process and continues until our focus and will are developed to the point where they are strong enough to bend the spoon that is our reality. We must be unwavering. We must relentlessly assert who we know ourselves to be and the life we know truly belongs to us. We cannot allow the illusion of our circumstance to make us forget who we are. That is really all it comes down to:

Which is stronger? The illusion of our circumstance, or the power of our will and self-awareness. That is the game we are playing, the one specifically designed to guide us toward realizing our creatorship.

Our primary task in life is to know who we are and do the things that help us to refine and express ourselves. That's all. If we do that, we will eventually find ourselves living the life we dream of, the one that we always knew belonged to us because it's just an extension of who we are.

You are an eternal creator being of infinite potential, the only question is will you come to realize this in your lifetime?

Becoming a creator being in the Game of Life comes with asserting our will while also allowing the universal will to emerge as well, creating in concert with the energies of what presents itself in the field of our experience. This process is a dance, and like any great dance we have to feel our way through it. We have to flow with it, guide it, let it guide us and allow ourselves to become one with the process. Any great writer, performer, athlete, etc., knows that greatness comes through allowing ourselves to be a conduit of the process. That is co-creation in its highest form. Though it usually takes an inordinate amount of practice and preparation to get us to the point where we can adequately surrender to the power of the process and allow it to flow through us freely.

A conductor leads the orchestra, he's not running to each section trying to play the instruments. Everyone has their part to play and honoring the multifacetedness of the process is really what allows it to reveal itself, once we give the process the time and space it needs to unfold organically. Even if something is presented that looks like it's the opposite of what we desire, we must know that it is specifically designed to carry us forward to exactly what we seek to realize.

Character = Story

In the Game of Life, the reality we experience depends entirely on the character we're playing, just as any movie is determined by its main character. In the first act the story shapes the character, in the second act the character finds direction and determination so that in the third act the character can shape the rest of the story.

Being the star of our own life comes down to picking the character we want to be and then aligning our mindset and actions accordingly. Success is really just about becoming who we want to be in life and it's important to note that this is far more about who we are than what we have. First, it's important for us to understand why we choose to put ourselves in the background so often.

How is it so many of us are not even the star of our own story?

The character we're playing is inextricably connected to our self-worth and the stories and beliefs we've adopted from our past and current experiences. We get in life what we're willing to settle for, so a big part of upgrading things comes in raising the standards we have for what we believe we deserve and expect from life.

The next phase of the Hero's journey can only begin once we claim the thrown at the center of our experience, where life no longer happens to us it happens for us, to move the story forward. Most people just aren't aware of the story they're telling about themselves and their lives. Those who actively cultivate their narrative process discover the power to create themselves and their life. It's just most people are trained by social conditioning to remain safely within the box of what's considered normal or average, which they are taught to conform to and expect for themselves. Things like the average life expectancy, divorce rate, average income, etc. People often internalize these expectations automatically, and so their experience is confined to operate within those specific terms of reality without them even realizing it.

Dodging Beliefs

The truth is we deserve the absolute best life has to offer and how much we agree with that statement on both a conscious and subconscious level determines both the quality of our experience and the power we have to direct our life. You are the center of your universe, your whole world revolves around you. And this is true for all of us. Think of a ball, if I were to point to any area on its surface and say it's the center, it'd be true. Every point on it is the potential center, but not all points claim this potential.

We are each a facet of the divine creator experiencing itself on the physical plane and therefore there's absolutely no reason why we shouldn't have everything we desire. All we have to do is shed the beliefs and limitations we've collected that girder our creative power, enforce lack and make us feel like we deserve less than the best. And at the very least we need to recognize our innate power, potential and worth. Shedding our unserving beliefs is about recognizing every time a limiting thought or belief pops up, understanding why we believe it and then consciously deciding what we actually believe to be true for us. This will determine the trajectory of our life so it requires honesty and often the courage to take action and make the internal changes that will help us to progress through self-awareness.

For the longest time I wanted to write this book, but that obnoxious little voice we have that mutters unhealthy things told me I was nothing short of ignorant to think I had anything of real value to share with others, and so the pages remained blank and a dream unrealized. I like to imagine this voice as a bouncer in front of a club, who tells me I can't go inside even though I own the club and it's my birthday party. How ridiculous is that? This is your club and everyday is your birthday. We all have the power to really own our life, but most people are just renting. Own your life? Are you kidding— with the average cost of living, the average home price and the average wage? We should be so lucky to rent our life.

Our indoctrination says: "Aim low and take what you can get." Claiming the fullness of our creative power has everything to do with understanding how much we believe of that statement and identifying where exactly we're setting our sights too low. Let's not fool ourselves, there's at least one if not multiple areas of our life where we're settling for less than we deserve. The key is finding it, tracing its roots and figuring out what we actually believe to be true for ourselves now at our current level of awareness.

Beliefs are the behind the scenes programming that determine what we can experience in the Game of Life. It doesn't matter how diligently we try to create something, if it's contrary to a belief we have we will only wind up reinforcing it until we acknowledge it and through our awareness resolve it.

The process for doing this is simple:

Identify the belief.
Find its roots: Why we believe it.
Define what we actually believe.

I have a good friend who is a single mother. Now this is no ordinary woman; she's kind, smart and beautiful and there's absolutely no logical reason why she would ever be single. But she comes from three generations of single mothers and had no idea that this expectation had quietly seeped into her own beliefs about how life was likely going to play out for her. She developed this subconscious mantra that she didn't need anyone and could do everything herself and so she did for a long time. But eventually she tired of carrying a load that was never hers to carry in the first place.

Each generation passes along a bag, it either gets heavier or lighter depending on how well the ones before us did with the one they received. What's in your bag? Looking at our parents' bags and our childhood it's easy to see how things found their way in there but it's important to remember:

> We can always unpack.

I know a lot of people enjoy examples so here's another one: I have another friend who had a challenging childhood and didn't receive the support or attention he needed and so as an adult he began to use sex excessively as a way of receiving that approval and affection, he also used inordinately expensive clothes as a way to project his self-worth. A few years into this struggle he began eating and drinking to self-soothe because the way he was using sex was only causing him to feel even emptier, and so he was literally trying to fill the void. This affected his well cultivated physique which deteriorated to reflect his internal struggle and created this loop to numb the pain that this emptiness was causing.

Most of the issues that stem from our childhood are centered around feeling inadequate in some way, so we spend our lives trying to find ways to prove we're enough, or to forget that we feel this way in the first place. We do our best to discover ways to elicit a feeling of validation but inevitably it only feeds the void until which point we're hurting enough to want to find the root of the problem and pull it out. Not dealing with past trauma and childhood issues is like playing whack-a-mole; it just keeps returning in different areas of our life.

Evolutionary Stalemate

We all have the compulsion to want something to be better than it is and yet do nothing about it. Even if someone is doing great in life, personal evolution is an ever upward journey towards greater versions of ourselves, our capabilities, and our life. At certain points in our journey it's undeniable when we've reached a plateau, which requires an extra push to regain an upward trajectory. The real reason why many of us have not realized a greater version of ourselves or our life is due to one of a few reasons: We feel maxed out by the effort it takes to maintain our daily life, the thought of doing it seems more painful than not doing it, or we're just not interested in making any changes or additional effort.

Personally I make conscious concerted effort towards my betterment every single day, but there are still things that I know if I could just do them it would catapult my growth. Yet I find myself in this holding pattern that pretty much every person finds themselves in at one point or another, and some find themselves there for their entire life. It's frustrating to want to change something and yet to do nothing about it. How is it that most of us know exactly what it takes to become or achieve what we want and still never do it? Is it because we're lazy? Partially— but there's much more to it.

It's important to understand that we are all locked into a habitual loop, and that loop happens every day and eventually becomes our life. It takes some intentional doing to systematically replace that loop with a higher more beneficial version that better supports our evolution. And small changes go a long way, especially when we're just getting started.

But how can we change when just the thought of it is exhausting? We are hardwired to avoid pain far more than we are wired to seek reward, which is why pain and suffering tend to be the most (eventually) effective ways to breed personal growth. It's also the reason why we're designed to hide out and stagnate in our comfort zones. This same avoidance of what we perceive to be painful is what has us choosing frustration and dissatisfaction over effort. If we assess the change we want to make as being more uncomfortable than things staying the way they are, we won't make the change. It's typically only once we perceive the current situation as more painful than the change that we're finally willing to do it. This is precisely the reason why life at times has to pretty much implode before we're uncomfortable enough to finally do something about it.

Comfortably Numb

The greatest problem for us as individuals is that many of us have acclimated to being uncomfortable. We lull ourselves with binge watching, online games, eating, compulsive scrolling and self-medicate in a variety of ways just to rid ourselves of the very feelings that are meant to spur us to action. Those feelings are supposed to make us uncomfortable enough to find out what is causing us to feel that way and change it. Modern life is filled with ways to feed our rampant escapism and distraction which is just dulling the suffering; distracting us from the fact that we are not who or where we want to be in life, but give us a funny animal video and suddenly that existential malaise is temporarily imperceptible. And so an endless loop is created like conditioned lab mice pressing the feeder bar, refreshing those feeds.

Progress requires a combination of the willingness to make the effort, do the uncomfortable, plunge into the unknown, gather insight about our process and carry out the actions that will propel us into a future far greater than we imagine. For me, goals like waking up at 5am on the weekends are continually vanquished without a second thought. I do it throughout the week but just cannot seem to bring myself to do it on the weekends; even though I know it's the perfect time for me to write for a few hours before the distractions of day start to percolate. Yet current version of me is choosing to remain in bed every Saturday and Sunday morning, while the Pulitzer Prize winning version of me loves to get up before dawn to chip away at a masterpiece one page at a time. The key is to find a way to reconcile the two, inch by inch, day by day.

Gifts of our Lineages

There are two reasons why we choose the family lineages we incarnate into. Aside from our soul groups another major factor is our karmic bonds, which is really just the residual algorithm we're carrying in from our previous games. This can manifest as limiting traits, behaviors and patterns like addiction, conformity, poverty, mental health issues etc. Each lineage also has tools, talents, traits and skills associated with them and so we often agree to transmute their negative attributes so that we can claim the gifts associated with that particular lineage. Let's say we want to incarnate into an energetic line that is known to have an algorithm of innovation and creative genius but the shadow side of the densities they carry are addiction and mental health issues. So we sign up knowing both the risks and the rewards, it's just most of us don't have the understanding necessary to push through to resolving the challenges so that we may claim those gifts.

Once we understand that life is not just a menagerie of senseless chaos but rather an intricately customized program specifically designed for us to learn and grow, then the lens with which we see our reality begins to shift in a monumental way. As we come to realize that everything that's happening is for our benefit and operate solely from this perspective, we begin to engage in the game as a conscious player.

Everything that happens is meant to increase our lucidity in one way or another, but often for some of the sounder sleepers life has to get real loud in order to get the job done. Fortunately I'm a pretty light sleeper nowadays, taking the hints when they come my way. There are still some brief narcoleptic bouts but now when I lift my head up out of them there's a keenness in realizing that the game just got me. It just shined a light on a weak part of my game and now I'm going to work on it so the next time around I've patched up that leak and hopefully transmuted into an asset instead of liability, because that's what great players do.

The Storyless Monk

A great shift comes once we realize that the story we are telling is what causes all of our suffering and that it's typically focused on the perspective of the past or future. When we start to feel defeated or worried it's usually because we're looking too far ahead and get disheartened by how far we appear to be from the top of the mountain we're climbing. If we take the path one step at a time it starts to become a lot easier: one day at a time, one moment at a moment time. At a very challenging and accelerated period in my path I was doing 12–16-hour days on five hours sleep, day after day. I would find myself wondering if I possessed the strength and will to get through the day. Then a higher version of my inner dialogue reminded me that I don't have to get through the day, all I have to do is get through this moment, and surely I have enough in me for that. When we narrow our focus to only the singular task that is before us the way becomes much simpler and we are able to fulfill our tasks.

I found that existing in this period of perpetual exertion helped me to realize something, many things in fact. I began to anchor into a more Zen approach to my experiences and the challenges they contained. This came through transcending the story about my experience. Fundamentally it just is. If our experience of the physical world is in fact a cerebrally generated illusion as quantum physics asserts and I believe it is, then reality is just blank energy that is transforming based on our narrative.

The story is just the surface illusion we tack onto our experiences and in any moment we can plunge beneath the surface of our experience to a deeper realm of infinite potential. The energy that forms our experiences is fundamentally blank until it is imprinted with our story of it, but this is just our narrative of the surface. I started realizing that one can transcend our surface stories at will by plunging beneath them to the inherent isness of the moment. It is in this state of beingness that the things of the surface world quickly recede and from this space comes a knowing that the story we have commands the surface, and in doing so it can manipulate the ability our essence has to express its potential. So I began to explore the ability we have to restore our power and vitality by plunging beneath the surface and into the wellspring of eternal beingness.

There is one fundamental energy that animates our universe and all of creation; the primordial source energy from which all things are crafted. This energy in its fundamental form cannot be reduced in any way, it is pure and infinite. What we are doing when we plunge beneath the surface of our experience is connect to the essence of this prime energy that is animating all of creation. This prime creative energy is happy to provide us with the privilege of also being a creator and so it is designed to transform its surface in accordance with our will, which is transmitted to it through our dialogue; both the internal and external narrative we are running that forms the story we are telling about our personal experience of life. The more we cultivate our narrative and learn how to relinquish the parts of it that are not serving us, the more we come to realize our creative power to craft our experience.

It is the story we have about what we are experiencing that causes all of our joy and suffering. So if we withdraw the story we have about our experience, especially a challenging one, we strip away the power of its subjectivity and return it to a neutral happening. I never understood why Tibetan monks would sit on big blocks of ice for hours on end, that is until this understanding dawned on me: They are training themselves to transcend the surface and plunge into the realm of the infinite. That is what practices like cold plunges and ice baths are doing, it's a visceral way to train ourselves to transcend the surface of our experience. Doing this refines our ability to unembed ourselves with the surface and therefore claim the power of Creatorship that lies at the center of our beingness.

The Illusion of Time

There's a reason why life expectancy is drilled into the minds of the collective; as a means of enforcing a consensus reality of predestination. I don't believe in age. I don't really believe in time outside of its organizational purpose. Time is an illusion and to rectify this I believe we should look upon time as cyclical rather than linear. If I didn't live in a society that constantly reinforced the construct of time, all conception of time would fall away. I imagine if I lived in the wilderness somewhere all that would remain of time is not really time at all but the simplicity of natural cycles. There would be morning, afternoon and evening and the changing of the seasons and that would be about the extent of time, just a simple and natural cycle.

Time is a construct created by humans as a means of orientation and planning and is useful in those respects, but the idea of accruing years both personally and collectively I find to be totally superfluous. I find the concept of age to be nothing short of ridiculous. Have you noticed that being forty now doesn't look anything like it did twenty years ago? Why is that? Time is not having the same effect on us that it once was, and this is because many of us are disengaging from the construct of age and so its grip is loosening because our belief isn't giving it the power it once was.

Time is an illusion. There is only ever this moment and the more that we reside in this moment the more our being gets to claim eternity as its natural state. The game is not intended to have a set duration, we are meant to play the game for as long as we like until we decide we're done playing, this is as true for the Game of Life as it is for every other game. The time limit is only there as a means of control; the Constrictive Illusion that keeps the masses on a strict track of pressure and predestination.

Even now as I write this, I just so happened to come across some online content in the form of a movie clip of Eddie Murphy saying that all we have is seventy-five years. Frankly it's asinine, served to us as fact and those who buy into it are in for a bleaker ride than those who don't. If you need help departing from the constructs of standard reality remind yourself that it's aimed to govern the sleeping masses and those considered to be average. To me logic suggests that the longer we're playing a game the better we should be getting at it or we're clearly not playing it right. And this applies to all of our states, including our physical, which like everything else in life is a direct reflection of our inner world and what we're consuming on all levels of body and mind.

Whatever you believe to be true, will be true for you. We can create our own rules in life which are all built around what we think about "the way life is." These beliefs are developed by the way life has been and how we think it's likely to play out for us in the future, most of which is based on our social conditioning and how we see it play out for those around us. Those who achieve great things in life achieve them because they live life on their own terms and are completely unwilling to accept the limitations of their circumstances which is what allows them to push past the illusion of it and into victory.

When I think about a memory or a dream I've had both feel the exact same, with the same level of "realness" and there's never any time associated with them. I might try and project a time but it's just a vague feeling of that or then.

When I think back on the time that has passed, it doesn't really feel like it has, it feels like this morning is of equal distance as something that supposedly happened decades ago. It's either now or not now. Initially I thought our internal growth is the real measurement of time passed but it's not because when I recall anything, even from childhood, I'm never actually that version. It's always experienced from a seemingly unchanging aperture of awareness, meaning there's really only ever the awareness behind the experience.

Even when I try to think back to my daughter as a baby, I can't really because it feels like this is the only version I've ever actually known, the idea of her as a baby feels like a wisp. If I had no photographs I would have almost no recollection of it and the same is true when thinking of my parents from when I was child. All of this is too illusive to adequately explain but it's all tied to the truth that there's really only now. Everything that is not happening now recedes and as it does its realness dissipates just as a dream does, like a wave returning back to the ocean.

I believe that all players in the Game of Life will evolve out of having long term memory, sooner rather than later. There will still be some long-term recall but the portion of the brain once used for long term memory will become a small fraction of what it once was and this is for a few reasons. It is no longer necessary for the evolutionary purposes it once served in the hunter-gatherer way it was designed, technology now ensures we rarely need to use it as our phonebooks, timers, and calendars are there to do the legwork for us. Also, our minds are now constantly bombarded with non-linear stimulus which will shape the way our brain grows and evolves. This will give way to two modes of operating: The first mode is a more erratic and unfocused functioning, the second more refined mode will provide a more multi-dimensional way of understanding and being. The key differentiator will be the person's ability to focus and engage in their experience with curiosity and awareness.

It is clear there exists a cycle of unfoldment we call time, but it is cyclical not linear and therefore it absolutely does not have to translate into the deterioration of our health or vitality. The only reason it does is because we are thoroughly conditioned to believe that growing old is just the way it is. What if it's not? What if our evolution is commandeered by the ingrained belief that time is our master? If the Game of Life is in fact just a simulated virtual reality, how ridiculous would the concept of aging be? The two biggest ways we relinquish our power and potential is through believing the lack and limitations projected onto our experience. If we can escape the framework of time in the manner in which it is used to control then we will be free to realize our potential in ways the generations before us never dreamed of.

Now more than ever we must begin to cultivate a willingness to look at things differently and entertain the possibility of new perspectives. There is a wonderful musing that asks which is longer: 1,000 years where absolutely nothing happens or changes, or a few days during which 1,000 events occur. This is meant to point out that time is primarily measured and perceived through change. So if there is no change then how could one ever measure or perceive its unfolding? When nothing is happening it feels as though time isn't really moving and in the same way in periods when there is a great deal of change time feels to be unfolding at an accelerated pace.

Another thing to ponder is this: Looking at time from a past and future standpoint, the moment we put aside the concept of years the past and future become far less defined and delineated. The periods that most stand out as markers of past, present and future are generally distinguished by changes that shift the way people live. This is usually marked by inventions, historical events and systemic innovations that change life in a monumental way: Electricity, the automobile, industrialized food, the internet, smart phones, A.I., these are all markers that can be used to define specific eras and that era would continue until the next major marker presents itself.

Looking at time as cyclical rather than linear, we could view the collection of past, present and future as a clock, with each major era represented as a number as well as the intervals between the numbers. Personally I feel like this helps to reconcile the idea that the past, present and future are all happening simultaneously. Our vantage point, the position we occupy on the clock would determine what we consider to be past and future. Each era is the present point for that position on the clock and also the past and future point for the one on either side of it.

Keeping this in mind, is it possible then that the Ancient Egyptians are really a civilization from the future who sent these relics to our timeline as a way of trying to share their knowledge? Literally drawing it out for us in hopes we would figure it out and ascend in our human evolution. And maybe the pilgrims were galactic refugees fleeing from a tech ravaged world who sought to start over from scratch in hopes of getting it right this time, and every person who tried to bring technology into the "new world" was incinerated.

These thoughts are purposefully meant to seem outlandish but it's important to entertain these ideas because it can help open us up to possibility and help shift what was once an immoveable perspective of things. What if each generation's history is just an experiment to see how different world events affect the progression of humanity's evolution? Maybe we are highly advanced beings that decided to come to this specific era just to see how quickly we could raise it to another one: The ultimate evolutionary game.

Eras previous to this one projected the year 2000 to be the wave of the future, full of flying cars, robots and recreational space travel and now a quarter of a century later we are still yet to reach any of these milestones. Perhaps that is because the year we are in holds little significance and what really matters is the era, and understanding the distinction between the two is what will allow us to continually shift to greater evolved eras. The introduction of A.I. is a huge signpost that we're now entering a new era and with that all of the innovations and inventions of that era will also become manifest. This brings both uncertainty and excitement as we hurdle toward a new era brimming with possibility. It is also important for us understand what this new era looks like for us on a personal level because having a clear picture of it will help us to align ourselves to it.

Programming Parameters

When we enter the Game of Life, we do so by using a default character which is the equivalent of being a background actor just to get on the movie set. Our default character plays its roles and is programmed with all of its necessary parameters: personality attributes, backstory, major life experiences, etc. All of which is designed to eventually enable us to ascend to the higher levels we've set as our goal.

Personally I believe that creation is finished and that all possibilities and potential outcomes exist within the program library. We technically have the ability to access and experience any of them but due to the nature of personal resonance, limiting beliefs and patterned choices we have access to a very small spectrum of those possibilities. And through our habitual loops we further limit that ocean of infinite possibility into a miniscule sliver of potential experience available to us. Our habits, of which none of us are immune, are the biggest track of predestination that we are all on. A good life is built by making good decisions and the quality of our daily loop is what determines the bandwidth of experience available to us.

Some years ago I was tasked with driving my Godson home from school and as we navigated our way through some of the most horrendous traffic I'd ever stewed in, inch by inch I huffed and scoffed my way towards an aneurism. He addressed me from the back seat with a special blend of surfer-kid zen reminding me to "enjoy the journey" and after a long pause, in coup-de-grâce fashion he added that "traffic is just a state of mind". Checkmate.

Whatever emotional state we're in at a given moment emits an electromagnetic frequency that tunes us to the corresponding type of experiences. Now it's important to note that there's a difference between our daily experiences and the life changing events we call core experiences. We typically don't attract a core experience because we're emitting a certain emotional frequency. Those things are generally coded into our path like a cosmic game of shoots-and-ladders. We choose to experience specific advantages and challenges because of the insight and character development that experience will bring as a result.

Another thing to take into consideration is that life is an intricate co-creation process with other people who have also made their own choices and sometimes we agree to cause or experience a hardship so that someone else can grow by experiencing the lessons they need to and in that process we too will extract valuable lessons and experiences as well. Once we come to terms with the idea of choosing our experiences in order to serve our greater evolution and the evolution of the collective, we start to interact with our experiences differently, especially the difficult ones. We can often see the benefits that a hardship has brought us in retrospect and sometimes the greatest blessing is not getting what we thought we wanted at the time.

Once we understand that everything that happens is meant to support our personal growth, we begin to realize that everything is for our benefit and the sooner we identify what that lesson or benefit is, the sooner the obstacles we encounter dissolve. Only once we're consciously mining for the lessons and benefits in our experiences does the game really change. We initialize it in a whole new way, actively playing instead of it just running, hoping we'll realize what's going on and pick up the controller. We all have experienced things too awful or ridiculous to be true and all that we can really do is allow it to help us to grow and evolve.

Evolutionary Algorithms

It would benefit us greatly to look at our personal evolution from a more technological standpoint. On a sub-quantum level our energy is essentially just an algorithm, one that is constantly coding and communicating with the program field it exists within and as it does it refines and transforms.

When my daughter was just a baby and learning to talk, one of the things she would say to me repeatedly is "ny-ny-ny". This transformed into "nine-nine-nine" and later into "zero-zero-nine-nine-nine". This series of numbers was her name for me, to the extent that my mother would playfully refer to me by it as well. When she got old enough for me inquire why she called me 00999 she told me that that is how she found me when she was coming here. Her response put me back on my heels, but being just a toddler at the time that was the extent of the details I was able to get from her. Midway through the age of three she stopped calling me by the portion of my universal signature she had once remembered, but it always stayed with me as so fascinating, a little glimpse into how things are seen on the other side of the veil.

Within the algorithm that comprises our individual essence are our core codes; the quantum translation of who we are in our prime expression. Through trauma and repeatedly patterned experiences we can come to develop rogue code, code that compromises the overall integrity and effectiveness of the whole algorithm.

I imagine on the other side of game, the level of our energetic evolution can be very clearly seen in the algorithm we carry. How much have we simplified it and removed the anomalies and rogue code, carrying only the essence. Are we carrying 300 lines of incoherent programming? Or is our energetic algorithm a short and sweet collection of core essence codes. The more condensed our personal equation, the more power it has.

The people who are constantly tossed about by their experiences are because they take on the encoding of their experience as their own. This makes them a magnet for experiential code which essentially shields and blocks their essence codes from being projected into the field of experience. They are just a big ball of what happened instead of an emanation of their prime essence. That is the key difference between someone who has realized themselves as a creator being in the game of life and someone who is sleepwalking their way through the collective dream.

Why mindfulness, introspection and meditation are so invaluable to the evolutionary process is because they help to clear away the accrued junk code, allowing us to consciously debug and clarify our energetic algorithm. In doing so it is more powerfully received by the field of our experience and as a result we come to realize the influence our clarified energetic code has on the world around us. Doing the inner work is essentially just debugging our coding to restore integrity, clarity and quality to the algorithm we carry.

This perspective helps to give us a very objective understanding of what karma actually is. Karma is not a tally system of punishment and rewards; it is simply the energetic algorithm we are carrying with us from lifetime to lifetime. And each time we enter the Game of Life it is for the sole purpose of balancing and refining our energetic code through experience. This is what is really happening beyond the surface of our experience, a refining of our algorithm. When we initialize the Game of Life it analyzes our code and intelligently designs the path that will best balance and refine it. We review the plan, make any necessary adjustments, sign our waivers and contracts, and cue the crying baby.

Pursuit of Happiness

An important part of finding fulfilment in life comes after we understand how our desires can often lead us further from realizing them. There's a reason why the term manifestation doesn't appear anywhere else in the book, primarily because it is a huge sand trap in the Game of Life. Now I understand that this is not a popular opinion to have by any means, and that is because everybody likes a quick fix, add in a get rich quick scheme and you've got them panting.

Manifestation appeals to the lottery ticket buyer in all of us, the part that is conditioned to chase the dream of someday. This behavior keeps the wrong kind of hope alive, the kind that prevents us from fully living life right here and now. The law of attraction serves a valuable purpose in showing us the interrelatedness that our intention, expectation and state of being has on the field of our experience. For this reason it is important to have a clear picture of what we want in life and to dwell on it until we merge with it. But this is entirely about an inner state of being. We may genuinely want the spouse, the house, the yacht, and that's fine. We chose to have a material experience and material things are part of that. The thing about manifestation that leads us all astray is that it externalizes our happiness as the things instead of the inner state of being we associate with them and that is the biggest dupe of all. It is this mechanism that turns our perception of things backwards and we decide that only when we have these things will we have happiness, love, peace, freedom, fulfilment, and the list goes on.

All of our emotional suffering, all of it, comes from wanting things to be different than they are. Fundamentally what we experience just is, it is inherently devoid of meaning; just neutral stimulus. The experience we are having doesn't mean anything until we develop a narrative about it. A pregnancy, or breakup could be the best or worst thing to happen to us, it all depends on the story created around the experience. This is why reality is entirely relative. The experiences are the same but the narrative makes it unique to the individual, and our personal reality depends entirely on the story we craft around what happens.

Let's imagine for a moment that we are a cerebral vegetable; unable to form any thought or association about our external world. Winning the lottery, a terminal diagnosis, a marriage proposal, the death of loved one, the birth of a child, none of it would mean anything. In all instances the experiences are the same, the only difference is our ability to form a relationship to what we experience. This reveals to us exactly how we create our reality. What happens is not what matters, we just showed that our experiences are devoid of meaning until the mind intervenes and assigns one. So if we desire to be a creator of our reality, we do this by consciously cultivating what our experiences means for us, not from reaction but intention. If we can sincerely connect with our life, we will naturally craft a supportive narrative about it and eventually we will become master of our personal reality. Not because we can manifest whatever we want but because nothing that greets us on our path will change the overarching tone of the story we are telling, which for all of us is one of perseverance and self-realization.

There is very little media programming I allow my daughter to watch, but *I Love Lucy* is one of them. The other day Lucy remarked that you're either happy or you feel lousy and this prompted a discussion about happiness during which my now eight-year-old made an intriguing point: "Who wants to be happy all the time..." I asked her what she meant and she said: "I want to feel lots of different things, not just happy." Of course... Nobody came here to have a monochrome existence. The pleasure centers of the brain wire us to only seek out pleasurable experience, but the heart, the soul, wants to live in technicolor. We want to have all the experiences, taste all the flavors of being human because each emotion, each experience, touches us in different ways. It opens us, empties us, warms us, deepens us, nourishes us. Being human is messy but it is also incredibly beautiful, the real eternal kind of beauty; poetic, more felt than seen.

Happiness is the thing we are taught comes as a result of getting the things we desire to have in life, but it's the state that we truly desire not the things, we are just conditioned to believe the things are the only way to get to that state. Happiness is an illusion. It is a mental conception we chase endlessly which ironically brings us a lot of unhappiness in the process. What we are really chasing when we think of happiness is the desire to feel a deep sense of contentment with our self and our life. That contentment is already available to us in every moment regardless of our circumstance. The primary thing that robs us of our contentment is our mind's constant narrative, along with our relentless seeking, measuring and comparing. It's our story that we don't have what we want and that we won't be happy until we get it. It's exhausting. The thing we really want liberation from is not our circumstance, it's our mind and the looping narrative it has about us and our life.

Life is a gift, even when it's challenging.

Getting the privilege to wake up and have another day is a precious opportunity. To live life, to exist in this world, is a gift. To hear its sounds, feel its breezes, let the sun kiss our skin, to discover love and beauty in all the seemingly ordinary places it hides. But most of us don't live out in life, we live in our heads which can be a bleak form of solitary confinement. Sentenced to dwell on the fact that we don't have what we want, envying the people who do have it, all of which makes us feel like we're failing. This undoubtedly ensures that any potential joy we could have is pre-emptively annihilated.

We get two worlds to choose from to live in and each is an archetypal representation of both heaven and hell. Hindu philosophy believes the mind is maya, it is the illusory world. The mind breeds suffering and limitation while the heart is the expansive source of truth and knowing, it is what the Buddhists refer to as Vipassana, to see truly with clarity. Whenever we are suffering it's always because we are living in the stories of the mind. A cerebral vegetable could experience an immense amount of the sensation we know as pain and yet never suffer, because suffering implies a story built up around the pain. On the other hand, whenever we find ourselves in a state of joy or contentment it's a clear sign that we are living in the heart.

Our only task in life is to live it as fully as we possibly can, each and every day, regardless of how it appears to us on the surface. When we are in love with life, we already have everything. The gift is enough. Being in love with life doesn't mean that we are operating in a perpetual state of bliss. Growing up our neighbors were married for 70 years and they exemplified what enduring love truly is; the kind that has weathered every possible experience and still grows deeper. That is the kind of love that life wants from us, just as that is the kind of love we want.

The only way to truly live is to get out of our head. The mind bypasses our experiences by filtering it into a storyline while the heart directly experiences things as they are. All we have exists within this moment, but the mind commandeers this eternal moment and makes it just an incidental bridge between past and future. A place to regret and worry. But it's time to reclaim the present by exiting the mind and entering the heart, and we must repeat this process as often as necessary until the heart becomes our primary residence, our kingdom.

The Kingdom of Heaven is within the heart.

Our primary task in life is to live in the heart, present to this moment as fully and completely as we can be. In honoring this great task we consciously clear and integrate whatever keeps us from being in the heart consistently. The mind tells us things like we've failed because we're still not where we want to be and it whispers doubts that we ever will be. While the heart knows that what we want whole heartedly is our truth, it is part of who we are and what we came to realize. What we dream of is not separate from us, nothing is. The process of becoming our own highest expression is a natural unfoldment, like a flower blooms. The bud does not strive to be a flower, it is just one with the process. The flower allows life to flow through it freely, unobstructed. It doesn't look at its neighbors and feel like it failed, nor does it doubt its ability to bloom. It just exists in full and complete surrender to the rhythm of life.

Be like a flower.

But still the mind interjects, asking how we can speed up the process while the heart knows that all we can do is more fully allow the process that is already underway in all of us. But this does not compute with our collective conditioning to live only in the mind, to ceaselessly strive and do in order to acquire a collection of things that prove to us and the other minds that we are enough. *You are so far beyond enough.* We are just too confined by ordinary logic and reasoning to see the full scope of our essence and creative power.

The truth is we cannot speed up the process, we can only become more present to it by removing our resistance. Resistance is a mental creation; a judgment we have about something we feel or experience. We don't need to do more, we just need to become more available to the Life that sets itself before us to live. The mind might chime in with enumerations of all the things it wants to change; the sources of its dissatisfaction. If we have the power to change something that is causing us dissatisfaction then we most certainly should, we should improve all that we possibly can in our life. As for any seemingly unchangeable factors that remain we must accept them and we do that by understanding that the true source of our dissatisfaction is the story the mind is telling about them.

Acceptance of life as it is, isn't resignation, it is reclamation of the fullness of our experience. We can still make great effort to improve ourself and our circumstance, but it's important to note that if we don't first bring full awareness to our daily life we will lack the very thing needed to create a better one. Presence is the only way to harness our creative power, only then are we in a state that allows us to have more supportive and fulfilling experiences.

I have finally reconciled the estrangement I once had with the concept of destiny. It is the flower's destiny to bloom and so too we are here to experience a flowering of our own potential. Self-betterment is the only area of our life where we have any real influence, other than that this ride we are on is meticulously designed in divine perfection to carry us through the inner and outer experiences that move us along in our becoming process.

The biggest aspect of surrender comes with realizing that we are not driving this thing, try as we might to convince ourselves we are. We're not. Most people find this too uncomfortable to accept and so they use chronic doing as a way of creating a false sense of control over their life. The more control we need in our life, the less free we are to actually enjoy it. All we are asked for from life is to show up; to receive what's here right now instead of trying to escape it. The moment we do life opens up. Life is a relationship, hopefully the greatest relationship we will ever have, and like any relationship it is going to suffer greatly if all we do is try and control it and only focus on what we don't like about it. Once we are truly present, here for whatever the journey brings, that's when life opens up and the relationship we have with it flourishes.

In my personal journey I have expended a monumental amount of energy trying to do everything right; trying to white knuckle my way through making it happen. I finally realized how much constriction it was causing in my life and my self. This tension was usurping all of the joy that was available for me to extract from life. Now I'm taking a much different approach, relaxing into the surrender that comes with realizing that I was never really in control, that my destiny has been seamlessly carrying me forward since inception and the more I relax and surrender to the process the easier and more enjoyable the journey becomes. Now this does not mean I don't make effort, it means that all my action is just a natural expression of who I am as I move toward who I am becoming. It is far more about finesse than force. I no longer strive, measure or escape. My only task is to show up, and by that I mean be present to the moment that is set before me as fully as I can. It is all perfectly designed and will unfold accordingly, if I allow it.

I finally realize that life is not a test, it is a temple and now I treat it accordingly, and so each day my task is now to fill myself with as much peaceful reverence as I can muster.

Versions of the Self

Everything in life is inherently neutral. We convert our experience into personal reality the moment we develop a relationship to it, which is just our narrative of what we believe that experience means for us. The same significant life experience could happen to two different people and one person could make it the reason why they can't achieve something and the other could make it the reason why they will. Those two individuals will live entirely different lives as a result. In storytelling, the hero and the villain usually have similar backstories fraught with pain and suffering but the way they respond to it is what determines the character they play in the story.

Each major version of ourselves lives their own version of life which is left behind when that phase is completed; be it our childhood version, college version, married version or our supremely lost version. Some transitions are too ephemeral to pinpoint when exactly they shift while other shifts are distinctly marked by significant life events like graduating, getting married or having a child. Version shifts happen when life as we know it changes. Like a hermit crab we inhabit the shells of different versions of ourselves throughout our lifetime and if we ever find ourselves uncomfortable in life it's probably because we've outgrown our shell and it's time for a new one. Each version comes with its own phase of life and bandwidth of experiences, so if we are looking to change the quality of our life we're going to need to swap shells.

Freedom is Choice

The most common human desire is to have more personal freedom, which is really just a desire to expand the range of choices and experiences available to us. We think it's money that will expand our choices, but nothing expands the bandwidth of choice and experience greater than a shift in our mindset. Many people feel like they don't have the power to change things and though we may not always have control over what happens, we always have the power to choose how we relate to the situation and decide what it means for us. It's not what happens that matters nearly as much as our response to it. We always have the power to determine what our experience means to us, which forms the framework of the story we're telling and the reality we're experiencing.

No matter where we are in our life, no matter our situation, there are countless examples of people who've transcended remarkably bleak circumstances and realized a far greater life. And each and every one of them is proof that if they can do it, so can we. If Helen Keller, both a deaf and blind woman in the 1920's can find a way to write 14 books surely we can achieve whatever it is we're looking to.

We are the only thing standing in our way from getting to where we want to be, but it's much easier for us to make money or circumstance the reason why we can't do it. And we do this because we're afraid we won't succeed, so most don't even try. I don't believe in the concept of failure but if I did the only form of failure is not even trying. We miss every shot we don't take and in the end we wind up regretting the things we didn't go for far more than the things that didn't pan out.

True freedom comes with taking responsibility for the role we're playing in our story. We so often focus on how other people or circumstances affect or limit us and this is how we give our power away. Claiming the highest role we'd like to play in life requires us to take charge and play the game as we see fit, instead of just making do with the role that comes with the situations we're given. The key to success is simple: It's having a clear vision of what we want to accomplish and making consistent, often relentless effort towards attaining it until its realized.

Many people feel like they're stuck in their current circumstance with no way to change it. We nearly always have a choice to change things but what we often do is weigh our options and choose not to change it. The main reason people choose not to change something they really want to is that they've evaluated the change to be harder than just leaving things the way they are and so they *choose* for things to remain the same. This is the reason why New Year's resolutions are vanquished by the millions and it's the same reason why people stay in unhealthy relationships and work jobs they don't like. It's not that they don't have a choice; it's that they've assessed the difficulty of making the change as too hard and so have *chosen* for things to remain the same. If we're not changing something then we're choosing it. The real illusion is that what appears as the more difficult path is generally only more difficult initially and is actually the much easier and more fulfilling one in the long run.

Another reason why people resist making the change they want is because they've embedded their circumstance as part of their identity, so the idea of changing it makes them feel like they would lose everything. Those who do eventually make the change, generally only do so once it's gotten to a point where the current situation has become far too difficult and the change becomes easier than having things remain the way they are. All big change requires a loss of the familiar and the comfort of predictability, and it's this element of the unknown that has people stuck in stalemate.

If something's not working, choose something different. Don't get comfortable with being uncomfortable. If something doesn't feel right, be proactive and make it better. This is your life and it's only going to be as good as you're willing to make it.

Most people's biggest desire is for more personal freedom, this often means making the transition to a career they are passionate about. Passion is a primary ingredient if we are hoping to find a means of creating the independent wealth that so many of us desire. It's important to note that the amount of money we currently make is directly proportionate to the amount of value we bring to others. So if we follow our passion and enrich the lives of others in our own unique way, our wealth will increase proportionately to the contribution we're making. It is also important to note that money is a bi-product of existing in a self-empowered state and passion has a lot to do with facilitating that in the long term.

Family Money

In my observations I have noticed that most people's relationship with money is usually a direct extension of how supported they felt in their formative years. Do we believe that being supported is a natural part of life, that it's safe to trust in life and those around us? Because those are the beliefs that directly determine our earning power. Money is a bi-product of feeling capable and empowered and it is very clear to see how this pattern does or does not manifest in those around us.

Money is an outward manifestation that tends to be proportional to the level of entitlement we feel that we deserve to be supported. This is programmed subconsciously through our closest relationships which we in turn project onto things like money, love and life in general. How much we believe that life has supported us correlates directly with how much money we're capable of bringing into our life. Even wealthy people who have had an unsupportive upbringing develop all sorts of unserving patterns that create these money leaks and some people downright hemorrhage it, and all because they grew up believing they were unworthy of the support they needed.

An apt example of this are two friends of mine, a brother and sister I will call Charlotte and Richard. Their parents were frosty elitists to say the least, why they would ever have children was an absolute mystery to everyone. Each child had a dedicated au-pair since birth whose job it was to raise them until they we're old enough for boarding school. Charlotte went through practically every top-tier boarding school there was, being expelled from nearly all of them, while Richard was more eager to try and win his parents over with good grades. Charlotte saw boarding school as the place where wealthy parents put their problems and so she committed herself to playing that role as convincingly as possible. They both confided in me that neither of them could remember ever once being hugged or even touched by either parent. I could see the weight they were carrying, this longing to be loved. Coming from a rather vast multi-generational wealth, when they reached the age of 21 each of them inherited 30 million dollars to do with as they pleased. Both spent a substantial sum on things that would project their value to the world, clothes, cars and the like. They also developed coping mechanisms to help them to forget this pain they were carrying.

For Charlotte it evolved into a remarkably expensive drug habit, and she ran through a good portion of her inheritance partying all around the world with an ever-growing entourage. While Richard spent his inheritance trying to buy love, showering women with an excessively lavish lifestyle, gifts and trips in the hopes that they would stay around long enough for him to convince himself that they loved him. He also invested in people he shouldn't have in hopes that they would reciprocate the support. By the age of 35 neither of them had a penny to their name and it makes sense because money (like everything else) is just energy, which we program with expectations we have about how our world will support us based on how it has in the past. It's easy to see the relationship we have with it, and once we understand the relationship we have to something we have the power to change and improve it.

What it all comes down to is which mode our formative experiences set us to: Survive or Thrive. Wealthy people can be set to survival mode just as those raised without wealth can be given what they need to thrive in life, it's not as black-and-white as we may like to think. There is only one group of people who are seemingly exempt from this logic, and they are the individuals whose survival mode experiences served to light a fiery passion in them to thrive in spite of their upbringing and circumstance.

Our formative years are but a chapter in the story we are telling about our life and once we become aware of how those experiences have shaped the story we are telling and how it's continuing to affect us and the results we receive in our life, we begin to discover our ability change it.

For every person who feels like they have a less than ideal relationship with money, others, or life in general they can shift this perspective by making a point of recognizing the gifts they already have. The warmth of a home, good health, the food we have to eat, a caring friend, whatever we are blessed to have in our life, we must make a point of recognizing it until we can cultivate a deep sense of gratitude. The more we acknowledge the ways that we are supported in life the more we are wiring ourselves to thrive.

A willingness to serve others, be it friends, family or the less fortunate is another invaluable way to put things into perspective and bring both fulfilment and prosperity into our life. By supporting others we prove to ourselves that the world is a supportive place and so more support, luck and auspicious happenings find us.

Charlotte is someone who took this suggestion to heart and spent over eight months in Africa building schools and clean water systems and in doing so she received the genuine love and appreciation she had yearned for her entire life. She returned a different person and now lives a happy and fulfilling life as a successful visual artist in New York City. Richard also committed to resolving his core patterns and as a result he found a woman who truly loves him and has built a big beautiful family with her. He now finds great healing and purpose in being the loving father every child deserves to have.

The journey from survival to thriving is an opening of our energy channels from a constrictive to an expansive mode of expression and experience. Lack is a constrictive state which is why people in a constrictive financial state tend to use constrictive words to describe it. They may say that they're strapped or that things are really tight right now, all are signs that point to how the energy is flowing in the relationship dynamic they have with that thing.

Wealth is an expansive state of expression and experience, one that is flowing, wide and open. Lack and wealth are states of mind and being which transfer to all of areas of our life be it love, money, health or life in general. If we wish to realize greater wealth in our life, we need to find ways to put ourself into an expansive state energetically. Gratitude and generosity are invaluable facilitators in this process and those who embody these qualities have already discovered a great wealth that will only continue to be added upon.

You: Version 2.0

The reality we are currently experiencing is a direct result of the character we're playing. The only way to have a new version of reality is to embody a new version of ourselves, because our current reality belongs to the version of us who is experiencing it. We can recall past versions of ourselves: our childhood version, high-school or college version, each version we play in life has a specific set of circumstances, cast of characters and world in which it operates and only once we are no longer playing that version does that world recede with it.

Trying to have a new reality with an old character version is like trying to bring a checkers piece to a chess game, same board but entirely different game. It doesn't compute because our current version of ourself is tethered to the current reality it is experiencing. It is designed as an evolutionary pairing system; they belong to each other, making neither of them transferrable.

The only way to upgrade our life is to upgrade the version of the character we're playing. How evolved the version is determines a lot about the quality of what we're able to access and experience in our life. In reality everything is made of blank energy, infinite in its potential, and when that energy comes within a certain radius of our individual field it morphs to conform to our personal game within the larger collective game that humanity is playing. So as we navigate our world the blank energy of the interface morphs around us to correspond with where we're at in both our current phase of development as well as our emotional state in that given moment.

The expectations we have are a big part of what narrows and limits what can and will be delivered to us because the game's interface is programmed to uphold the story we're telling and keep the narrative running. So whatever we believe to be true, the field of our experience is programmed to deliver to us the things that reflect those beliefs and narratives in order to keep the game going. Understanding this key point is what allows us to claim the power we have to create our life, which has everything to do with the story we're telling about it.

The field of our experience is designed to present us with the circumstances that provide the support, opposition and revelations built to aid us in our evolution. As much as we'd all like the awakening process to be like the soft fabled kiss of *Sleeping Beauty* which allows us to open our eyes reborn; in reality none of us are such delicate sleepers and so we often require nothing short of an air-raid to get our attention. Part of ensuring life doesn't need to get loud just to get us to look comes with learning to tune into the subtleties being communicated and reflected in the patterns and details of our experiences. We must understand that everything that triggers us to fall sleep is a gift, shown to us so that we may discover and refine a weak point in the default way we are showing up to life.

The other characters in our experience also operate on the same principles as the rest of the interface which means they too are comprised of blank energy programmed to morph based on both the role they've been contracted to play as well as the input and electromagnetic signatures of what it encounters. The moment we are fully present with person or situation we successfully unlock the ability to access a much greater dimension of experience.

The reality we are currently experiencing is a direct result of the character we're playing and the only way to a new version of reality is to embody a higher more evolved version of ourself. The reality being experienced belongs to the character experiencing it, they are inextricably linked together. So the only way to upgrade one is to upgrade the other and this is done by upgrading the loop we're living each day in both our mind and our world, as well as bringing more awareness to our experiences.

Character Selection

Our character version is constantly changing whether we're aware of it or not, and conscious participation in the process greatly improves the results we receive. Anytime we experience a substantial shift in our life it is either the result or cause of a shift in character versions.

Version shifts are a natural part of the rhythm of life. We are constantly refining our identity through the meanings we assign to our experience as we narrate the story we're telling about our life, and in every moment we're reinforcing or altering our character in some way. Sometimes an entirely new character is presented for us to play, like becoming a parent for instance. Each character version is multifaceted and has a depth available to us beyond its roles. And it's always changing, though some more willingly than others.

Our first character is the one we inherit, the one we're born into as a means of getting into the game, which is comprised of all the things we've programmed and collected as we slept-walked through a game we didn't know we were playing. In order to step into a new version we must first shed the old one like a snake sheds its skin. Now this isn't about pretending to be something else, it's about shedding what is preventing us from expressing who we truly are. This is liberation, rebirth, resurrection, all of that. All of the great alchemists throughout history understood that resurrection is an allegory of awakening. Rebirth is the process we are undertaking right now, as we step into a higher version of ourselves and our life. Our first character version was simply everything we needed to experience to get us to this point right now as we anchor into the knowledge and power we have to consciously create the rest of our experience.

Personally I had to the do it all backwards in order to realize the process. I had built four rather successful companies by the age of twenty-five, but inevitably I discovered I was building an empire on quicksand and its downfall led to an unconscious change in character and with it came an entirely different reality. I went from being a successful entrepreneur living in a glass house in Bel-air, to living in a hovel of a studio apartment with one barred window, right next-door to a men's shelter. I was disenchanted with life and struggling with isolation and addiction and like many, needed to hit rock bottom before I'd wake up to my ability to choose a new version of myself and with it a new life. The one I chose was utterly determined to figure out how to turn things around and so I poured all of my energy into discovering how everything works; the body, reality, all of it. And the information shared with you here is the fruit of that quest.

We all have the power to choose a new version of ourselves at any moment which will come with its own reality, set of characters and experiences. The change may appear daunting but the effort it takes to change is far less energy than it takes to remain deeply unsatisfied with the way things are.

Crafting the Self

The foundation of every character version is its identity and self-image. Many people would like to change their self-image so that they can become a greater representation of who they really are, but most often this cannot be done directly because trying to only creates resistance and winds up reinforcing the very thing we are attempting to change.

The most effective way to create and sustain change is by focusing on introducing the positive rather than removing the negative. This is known as the crowding out technique, by introducing more positive we naturally reduce the space that is available to be occupied by the negative. Look upon the light of our awareness like the sun, whatever we shine it on will grow so it's imperative to focus our attention on expanding the positive.

There are generally three aspects that people want to change when it comes to the self-image: The physical aspect which is the body-image, the emotional aspect which is our internal narrative and the relationship we have with our self and our life, and the third is our self-belief which are the things we expect and feel we deserve based on our past experiences.

Now there are a few sand-traps in the game of life, areas where we can stumble into a seemingly inescapable loop that gobbles up all of our joy and energy, and a big one is being unhappy with ourselves. At one point or another most people have had a dysfunctional relationship with the state of their physical or emotional self and because it's a constant reminder that they are not who or where they want to be in life it's a source of a lot of unhappiness for many.

Just as we believe that if we had the money we desire all of our problems would dissolve, so too we peg our happiness on "if only we were in shape, or outgoing" then we would be and have all the things we're lacking. This is an inside job that is much more about our internal state than any external factor. It's about making the internal shifts that allow us to become a higher expression of ourselves, but this requires us to learn how to love and support ourselves unconditionally. When we feel free to be who we are, a radiance and vitality shines through. And the more we shine forth our essence the more natural it will become for us to be a radiant, fit and healthy version of ourselves.

The most important part of being naturally fit and healthy is having a better relationship with our body, our spirit and our lifestyle. It doesn't get any more fraught with resistance than dieting or counting calories. All we are doing is delivering highly charged commands to our body with every mouthful and even if we are eating healthy the underlying tone comes from an unhealthy place of resistance which creates the well-known phenomenon of celery eaters who can't seem to budge the scales regardless of what they do. This is just as much of a phenomenon as being able to eat whatever one wants and also not budge the scales, only it's anchored firmly in self-serving beliefs. If we act from a healthy place, we'll become healthy. But most of our actions around physical self-improvement are centered around trying to change ourselves so that we'll finally be able to physically display our worth, and so we chase an ever-moving target that only winds up reinforcing a feeling of inadequacy. The key is acting from a supportive place of genuine self-betterment.

We have all encountered someone who can eat whatever they want, as often as they want and still remain fit and healthy. I am happy to now consider myself a part of this group. I still always try to make high-quality decisions but I can also visualize working out and see the effects the next day. There are countless studies on mental rehearsal and the incredible effects it has on our body and mind. Now it wasn't always this way, there were times when all I'd have to do is glance at muffin and see the effects because the power of our belief is absolute. Everything in our experience including ourselves is made of blank energy, infinite in its potential, which receives our commands and transforms accordingly.

When I was studying psychology in university, there were multiple case studies which documented the ability some people with multiple personalities had to change their eye color based on the personality that was being expressed. These transformations were as significant as changing their eye color from dark brown to brilliant blue. Another remarkable case was a woman who was rendered cortically blind from an accident yet had some personalities with perfect vision, her brain scans showed that the moment she would shift into that version the visual cortex instantly started to receive signals again. It is truly astounding the things that unwavering belief can do. And as we begin to understand that we are inside a simulated interface designed to be programmed by our beliefs, the role we play in the results we receive is suddenly revealed to us.

The most important habit people must transcend in order to become healthier inside and out is to overcome the tendency for emotional eating, drinking and other self-sabotaging and self-soothing behaviors which cause us to feel temporarily better, then usually worse. We dissolve these patterns by understanding the root of why we developed the coping mechanisms in the first place. For most people it comes from unresolved issues that both cause and are triggered by a general dissatisfaction with themselves or their life.

Any significant weight issues are most often an external representation of the internal weight we are carrying. And for some who felt unsafe in their childhood weight gain can be an unconscious method of self-protection; believing that the bigger we are the less vulnerable we are. For chronic dieters and those with disordered eating, these patterns likely developed as a result of feeling unworthy of care and support because they were not provided those things in their formative years, and so they've adopted a need for rigid control and perfectionism to cope.

Our creative power is revealed to us once we truly understand that all of creation is crafted from blank energy which is programmed by our narrative and transforms accordingly. If we allow ourselves to enjoy something fully with great presence and intention, then it will nourish us regardless of what it is. The same goes for eating things we really can't stand because it's healthy for us, there has to be a happy medium for it to be a truly beneficial. There was a clinical study conducted on rabbits where the researchers were feeding them lethally high-cholesterol food. They were perplexed to discover that one group of rabbits was completely immune to what they were being fed. The researchers discovered that the clinical technician in charge of feeding that particular group of rabbits held, cuddled and kissed each rabbit every time she fed them; showing us that the state we are in when consuming something can supersede the thing being consumed.

The key to being vibrant, fit and healthy is simply acting from a supportive place of self-love rather than a place of resistance. This is the fundamental difference between dieting and nourishing ourselves with a supportive lifestyle. Once we start acting from a supportive place of self-love and self-acceptance, things come into alignment and so our body and our life reflect it.

The Game of Life is one of mind over matter and what we believe about what we're consuming is a primary determinant of the effects it has on us. There are countless studies on the power of the placebo effect. Recently there was a rather extreme study conducted by a group of doctors who took two groups of people in need of surgery: The first group had the surgery performed while the other group only had the incision made and were told they received the surgery. Their results are just one of countless studies showing the astonishing power of the mind.

Escaping Distraction

The Game of Life has hurdles we must overcome like numbing oneself with substances, food, shopping, sugar, sex and media content of all sorts. It's taken years for me to clear those hurdles, and some do pop up every once in a while but I'm aware of how I use them and abundantly so when it stretches into more than just an isolated incident. I've finally rid my home of TVs and have successfully detoxed from the news which I now realize is the stimulation equivalent of being waterboarded indefinitely. If you watch the news, for the love of sweet baby Jesus— please stop. There's little good that can ever come of it, it's just quietly siphoning our lifeforce energy, diminishing the will and programming all sorts of negative conditioning.

I can hear the mob now, my dad standing at the front of the pack: "Stop watching the news? I need to know what's going on..." The news consists very minimally of anything actually useful or relevant. Nearly all of it is rhetoric and propaganda meant to push an agenda of opposition, fear and uncertainty. The local news is just puppeting it in from the big boys and mixing in their own local brand of negativity, all of which is almost entirely useless.

The news finds its hook in giving people the false sense of security that comes from "knowing what's going on." Most of it has little to do with what's actually going on and much more to do with what to think and how to feel, which is usually some variation of low-level anxiety, uncertainty and fear for the future. "What's that—another recession is coming?" But not to worry they're letting us know eight months in advance so we can get good and worked up about it while we change our investing and spending habits so that we actually create one. All this programming does is create a very bleak and limited container to operate within.

Our energy and attention is our power, so a key to levelling up to a much greater version of ourself and our life is figuring out where our energy leaks are. The news is a huge one for many, sugar is another. Whatever the leaks are we should take a break for a week, preferably a month and see how much more effective we are at putting that energy toward getting what we want out of life. Anytime we encounter something that depletes our energy, whatever it is, its cause needs to be understood and boundaries created. Our attention is our greatest resource so anything that can gobble up hours of it unnoticed is a direct impediment to us realizing our creative power.

Escaping distraction means we have to break the habit of distracting ourselves from the discomfort of internal issues seeking our attention. A great player acknowledges and resolves any issues, then goes out and lives life. If it's something from the past that's trying to surface, we always have the power to change our relationship to it because what happened isn't nearly as important as the story we're telling ourselves about what happened. For example: It wasn't that the relationship ended, it was that its ending made us feel like we weren't worthy of the love we deserve. And so every time we dwell on the past we reinforce that feeling and belief by allowing it to hook into us and siphon our energy.

Understanding what quiet meaning we've given to what happened, especially the things we can't seem to get over is the key to being able to move forward because it's the meaning behind it that's really causing the suffering. It's not so much about what happens as it is about what we decide that means for us. Now if a problem is surfacing around worrying about the future, well that's like paying off a mortgage we don't even have. Could you imagine anything more ridiculous than paying off a debt you don't have? You sure can— It's called worrying about the future. Would it make sense for a player in any game to spend the entire game worrying about what's going to happen, vividly imagining all of the ways the game's not going to work out in their favor?

Sounds ridiculous, doesn't it?

The past and the future are the quicksand traps in the Game of Life and the real kicker is the more mental and emotional energy we feed them, the more we solidify their attachment to us as well as their recurring patterning. We can only play the game in the present moment so if at any point we find ourselves dwelling on the past or worrying about the future it's safe to say that we're asleep and the game is playing us.

Autopilot can be a good thing because it takes over whenever we're doing something habitual or living in our head. Autopilot is also incredibly helpful when someone does not possess the skills to fly the plane themselves. It also serves us in helping to conserve our energy by developing automatic patterns of doing things. Until we reach a supreme level of lucidity autopilot will remain a part of our game. Fortunately there's a way to use it to our advantage by developing a habitual loop that supports us in becoming a greater version of ourselves.

Once we reach a certain point in our evolution something quite remarkable happens and that is that autopilot transforms into flow. Harnessing the awesome power of flow allows us to feel supremely connected to our experience, and the more we learn to surrender to the power of it the more we're able to bring forth a remarkable level of performance, inspiration and effectiveness.

Personal Power

As a recovering perfectionist, I am all too familiar with the unwinnable game it is. Perfectionism is the coping mechanism of those who felt they weren't good enough and so they set the moving target of unreachable standards as a way to quietly reinforce their feelings of unworthiness. Most perfectionists did not receive an adequate amount of love or encouragement in childhood and so this is their way of over-compensating. They see their version of perfection as the way they will finally prove their value and self-worth to the world, but all it really does is leaves them rigid and unhappy. None of us are perfect and the real twist is that these broken and imperfect parts of ourselves often hold within them all of our untapped strength, power and genius.

We are all artists in one way or another and the greatest artists are great because they leaned into their pain, opened up to the broken parts of themselves and found strength and genius inside. Embracing ourselves is the only way that we can come into the fullness of our personal power and potential; realizing that our pain and struggle is the catalyst that helps us to find and refine our gifts.

We all know people who've had an average childhood, or a privileged or sheltered life and having never experienced much pain or struggle they lack any real depth. This is because you need pressure to make diamonds. So many great minds in every field have been able to tap into their suffering and create masterpieces, bringing forth things that change and enrich all of our lives. Only once we embrace ourselves fully are we able to truly harness our power. Discovering the depth of our talents comes with understanding that most of our gifts are often hidden in the messiness of the parts of ourselves that we try to hide or ignore. Conformity is one of the strongest social urges but only once we stop trying to blend in and focus our energy on discovering what makes us unique can we begin to claim our personal power. Everyone has something special to contribute to the world that is unique to them, but in order to discover what that is we have to lean into being ourselves as fully as we possibly can.

We could all benefit from allowing ourselves the opportunity to express ourselves more freely. It doesn't need to be perfect, it just needs to be real. There are so many singers who don't sing, artists who don't paint and writers who don't write because they've convinced themselves that they're not good enough. We must do the things we love, just for ourselves. If we are real, if we are fully and completely ourselves, people will respond to it because authenticity is a quality we all intrinsically gravitate to. Once we no longer reject those imperfect parts of ourselves, we start to experience the incredible power of our own wholeness. And once we're truly good with ourselves, that's when the game really starts.

Upgrading the Loop

The loop we establish as our daily life is what sets our bandwidth and narrows the choices and experiences available to us. This becomes our own personal autopilot, the default experiences we have like clockwork. As habit continually narrows that loop more and more, we start to feel the constriction of its monotony.

How we expand the bandwidth of choices available to us is by making new choices and experiencing the unknown. Taking a new route to work, trying a new coffee shop, talking to someone new, there are countless ways to simply widen the scope of new experiences available to us. The mind might resist this at first and this is because it only likes what it can predict, it's the prime enforcer of the loop we've created. We will always have a loop, it's part of the cyclical rhythms of life. Waking up, grooming, eating, sleeping, that is the framework of every person's loop regardless of who they are. Once we introduce a higher version of what we want to experience this process will be directed to work in our favor.

Understanding how we establish our loops is what allows us to build new ones. We're all given one 24-hour loop, which we repeat indefinitely until the game is over. The sum of our loops is our life. The character we're playing is an overall representation of the beliefs we have based on the meaning we've given the story of the past, which we integrate as our identity: This is what happened, which means this is who I am and how I expect life to be. This forms the bandwidth of the choices and experiences available to us and is further reinforced by our ongoing choices which either narrow or expand what is available to us in the future.

Many of us are going through the motions in 80% of our life because everyday we're running slight variations of the same loop over and over again. The only difference is that some loops serve us more than others. Our loops often become a constrictive reality: we think the same thoughts, sit in the same spots, travel the same routes, have the same conversations, eat the same foods, watch the same kind of content, go to bed and then do it all over again. The habitual loop we form is based on the identity of the character we are playing: the athlete, the single parent, the artist, the addict, the entrepreneur, are all going to have a very specific set of habits and routines that reflect the mindset and lifestyle of their version of that character.

The satisfaction we have in life is directly determined by the amount we are actively engaged with our experience. Many of us are just thinking our way through life, while being awakened is any moment where we've taken the mind out of the equation and are directly experiencing our world. We all oscillate between a thinking-centric state and a being-centric state all day long. The key is expanding our slivers of lucidity into more substantial periods which is where mindfulness and meditation are invaluable tools in building the muscle of being so that it may play a more prominent role in our daily life.

Our creative power is forever proportional to the amount of awareness we're bringing to our experience.

Tuning In

The reality we experience is determined by the electromagnetic frequency we are emanating, which matches us to the corresponding bandwidth of experience. There are two sides of the spectrum, the constrictive electromagnetic frequencies and the expansive electromagnetic frequencies. If our electromagnetic state is set to the frustration mode of experience, then we can be sure that it will align us to the corresponding spectrum of experiences and we'll likely catch every red light on the way to that appointment we're late for. Set to the love frequency? Then the road will rise up to meet us, songbirds will serenade, and magic will eagerly emerge from the ordinary and openly share its beauty with us.

There's a simple way to instantly connect to and shift the electromagnetic frequency we are emanating into the field of our experience. This is done by tapping into feeling behind our eyes. Initially we may not be able to distinguish a feeling but it's almost never neutral. We operate on either the constrictive or expansive electromagnetic bandwidth. Being in a deep meditative I AM state is likely the closest one could get to emitting a neutral frequency.

It's all in the Eyes.

Tapping into the feeling behind the eyes may lead us to internally inquire about our emotional state and it's incredibly beneficial to establish a dialogue like this with ourselves. This inquiry may provide us with an answer, or it may lead us to another sensation in the body. As I write this, I actually find myself on the negative bandwidth. It's the morning of Christmas Eve and there's some constrictive tension built up around all of the things I have to do to prepare. A nice deep breath helps to clear some of physical tension away but it's still there and acknowledging it is the first step to shifting it.

So how do we shift our frequency?

One effective way is to change the feeling we are projecting from behind the eyes. Here's an exercise: Imagine you're an actor filming a scene and your love interest just entered. You've never met before but it's love at first sight. You glance at each other, a little smirk crawls across both of your faces.

Can you feel a palpable shift in your electromagnetic state, and in the feeling being projected from behind the eyes? All good actors can tell the whole story with their eyes, and so too can you determine the story you're experiencing with the feeling you are projecting from yours.

Play around with this method to shift your states and explore the best ways to tap into the expansive range of frequencies. The simplest and most effective way to instantly shift states is to soften the eyes with a slight smile and anchor it with a contented breath. This can instantly shift us to the positive spectrum of experience for as long we can maintain it. And if we do notice that our state has drifted, we can reset it as often as we need to. Remember it's all in the eyes, and the way we're looking out into our reality and at others is the energy that is returning to us to create our world and the quality of our experience.

Setting Expectations

A lot of people want to change their beliefs but think it's a complicated process, when all it really comes down to is what we expect from life based on the level of quality we feel we're entitled to. Initially this is established subconsciously through how we were treated in our formative years as well as how we see life play out for those around us. If someone's family has a lot of blue-collar workers, academics, entrepreneurs or single mothers they are likely going to pattern these things into their own experience because logically we expect things to play out for us as we've seen it happen before. Our family, friends and relationships are by far the biggest factors that set the bar for us and quietly determine the things we believe are most likely going to happen in our lives.

The most important factor in upgrading the quality of our life is feeling entitled to greater things. We've set a bar, the standard for the quality we expect in every area of our life, much of which was initially set on a subconscious level but with awareness can be set consciously. We receive from life what we're willing to settle for and most people settle for far less than they deserve because they're afraid nothing better will come along. This is the reason why people enter and stay in unhealthy relationships, crappy apartments and dead-end jobs. We start to think it's our only option and that something's better than nothing, so we choose to settle and close ourselves off from all of the better options.

Life is a catalogue of items, people, and experiences, and our standards and expectations narrow that catalogue down to a very small and specific bandwidth of potential. Those who feel they're entitled to great things receive them because they have the confidence to refuse to accept anything less than the standard they've set. If we hold an unflinching, delusionally unwavering belief that things will turn out in our favor, they will. Our reality will bend to our will if it's strong enough. It might take relentless persistence, but it can be done. We are handed examples of others who've done exactly what we're looking to do as encouragement to show us that if they can do it, so can we.

We get to choose the character and role we're going to play in the Game of Life, it's entirely up to us to determine the level of influence we'll have in this world and the mark we're going to make. And we do that by determining what success means to us and how we plan to attain it. Most people think they're stuck with the character they came with, or if they do step into an improved version it's still limited by the logic and standards of the last one. The truth is we're here to become an expression of our own highest potential and in order to do that effectively it requires continually upgrading ourselves. That is how we experience the full spectrum of what we're capable of becoming and in doing so open up to all that life has to offer.

Reality is a mirror. It can only echo back who we already are and what we believe we have. If we act from a place of having and giving, our world will reciprocate. Our experience is designed to constantly reflect us back to us, this benevolent arrangement ensures we have an endless feedback system that allows us to grow and eventually reap what we sow.

Imagine the universal field like the drive-thru speaker of a fast-food place. We say our order into the speaker knowing full well that we will receive it. We don't tell them how to prepare it, nor do we go into the kitchen and try and prepare it ourselves. We also don't just sit at the speaker and wait for it to magically appear. What we do is prepare to receive it by engaging in the process that has to unfold: First we decide what we want, then we state our order, next we go to where we need to pay, then we position ourselves where we need to be in order to receive what we asked for.

> The universe works in the same way.

The Hall of Golden Doors

Imagine you are walking down a long hallway of doors and the one at the very end is a golden door. You approach it and try to open it. The key is our frequency, the quality of the energy we emanate based on the level of energetic refinement we have attained up to this point. If we are a match, the door will open. When most of us try our hand at a golden door and it doesn't open, we assume that it's not our door when really it's not a no, it's just a not yet.

Now let's say we've been granted entry and enter through a golden door; we assume our dream life is on the other side but what we find is a hallway of twelve golden doors. Now what? Which one holds inside it the dream life we are seeking to realize? The key at this point is to focus on getting a very clear picture of what we are looking to call forth, connecting the feeling of it and then waiting to be internally guided to what matches what we desire. This is the co-creative process in a nutshell: A clear vision of what we intend to realize followed by periods of allowing ourselves to be led to it, allowing for it to reveal itself. Most people are trying to do both sides of creation. The "what" is our department, the "how" belongs to the universe. If we are trying to make something happen, we are most likely getting in our own way.

Allowing things to come together is a necessary and cultivatable ability of anyone on their way to self-mastery. There's a big difference between trying to make something happen and allowing inspired action to flow through us. Lending ourselves to be a conduit of the process and allowing it to reveal itself through us is the key to seeing it realized. The difference is a subtlety, a flow, an ability to take the hints and dance with creation. A lot of people try to will what they want through blunt force and sometimes it works but there's a much easier and more effective way of working with the energy that animates our physical world and once we learn how to communicate and collaborate directly with this cosmic field, we come to realize our position as a designer of our individual and collective game.

The key to building exponential momentum is finding something that we are passionate enough about to be obsessed with. Most people have a vague, lukewarm idea of what they may like to experience but it's the magnetism of our passion that draws us to that golden door. Obsession is a key ingredient. It's got to speak our language, be all we can think about and constitute a good portion of what lights us up and makes us come alive. Most people think that once they walk through that golden door *then* they'll feel that way, passionately alive, but feeling that way is how we find and open the door. The only way we can be a match for the door that holds the life that we desire is by being in that state now. How could we possibly open that door and merge with that version if we are not already that version? We must live as if it is already so, this is far more about mindset than anything else. Feel that way, think that way, act that way now, because that is the only way to find and open our golden door.

The Heart Unplugged

For many of us there comes a point in our life where we deliberately turn down the volume on our capacity to feel. This is done in a self-protective act because at some point something got to be too overwhelming for us to handle, or something cut too deep and we couldn't risk it happening again. It is at this point that we metaphorically unplug some of the connective cables so that the hard parts of life couldn't reach us so deeply anymore. The catch is that doing this also turns down the volume on all of the good things too.

For the last few years, I've worked diligently on being able to feel deeply again which was daunting because much of what floats to the surface are the unpleasant things we repressed because we just couldn't deal with them at the time. For me it was worth it to face and feel it all because it had gotten far more unsettling to feel like the happy moments in my life weren't able to really reach me deeply. I was happy on the surface but none of it was able to truly reach the heart because there was a clear disconnect between myself and my experience, so I chose to suffer in order to repair the connection.

We are all carrying emotional weight with us and the thing is the longer we carry it, the heavier it gets. The experiences that life brings to us can be incredibly difficult, but not dealing with those things makes their residual effect far more challenging than the initial experience. The number one unprocessed emotion is grief and the best definition I've heard is that grief is love with no place to go. Keeping this in mind we can then understand that it extends far beyond a feeling we have for those we've lost. Grief also applies to every time we had love to give and could not give it. This could be the love we had for an unsupportive parent, an unreceptive partner, ourselves, a failed business, an unrealized dream, etc.

The love we have for these things, whatever they are, could not be expressed for one reason or another and so this repressed love stays inside us and decays, and the longer it stays the heavier it gets. The only way to get rid of the weight we're carrying with us is to process it. We do this by taking note of the people, things and experiences that we have not allowed ourselves to grieve about and then sit with the feelings that surface around it. This is the only way to lighten the load we are carrying and in doing so we find more clarity and free up more of our energy, power and potential.

Often we feel like if we face or feel these things we'll be broken beyond repair, but it's far easier to just lean into it than it is to avoid it our whole lives. This is the only way to defragment ourselves and return our being to a state of wholeness. We do this by allowing ourselves to experience it, releasing the resistance that has built up around the idea of it, accepting it and just allowing ourselves to feel however we want to feel about it. This is how we reclaim our power, but it takes courage to do this.

Once we start doing this we usually feel lighter almost immediately, or after a good night's rest. Either way we can palpably feel the benefits of doing this inner work and as a result we become more willing to keep doing it. A healthier pattern emerges as we start to acknowledge when things arise or trigger us and then follow them so we may see it, sit with it, and accept it, and in doing so eventually resolve it. Many of the people who do this inner work also start to notice that they lose physical weight as well, as the outer body is a direct reflection of our inner state and so a lightening of one state often naturally translates to a lightening of the other.

Anything that triggers us is a gift because it points directly to something that is controlling or restricting us behind the scenes. The only way to reclaim our power is by befriending the emotional dragons of our past through acceptance and acknowledgement. Acknowledge how difficult it was, acknowledge how unfair or painful, we must give ourselves the right to feel however we want to feel about it. To go within and say the things we never got to say to someone or to ourselves. To fall apart, and as we do the cracks of our broken aspects begin to seal themselves with gold.

Healing the Heart

Now it's very easy to tell someone to shed an old character like they would a dirty t-shirt but for a lot of people some of the wounds they are carrying can still feel deeply embedded. Those wounds all come down to the experiences we've had that made us feel loss, abandonment, rejection or inadequacy. We all have these experiences, the key is getting to the root of them by understanding what meanings we've given them and how this plays into the story we're telling about ourselves and our life.

I have a friend whose mother left him at a very early age which was his core wound, meaning it was the root of his feelings of abandonment and being unloved. As a result, he subconsciously patterned this dynamic into all of his relationships. One after another he dated emotionally unavailable women who wouldn't treat him well and would walk out on him abruptly. I generally would only hear from him whenever one of them would leave and he needed a shoulder. I tried to help him to see the pattern he kept repeating but he wasn't ready to see that he was just dating the archetype of his mother over and over again.

We need to be ready to heal in order to move forward. Many people prefer what's known even if it's unhealthy because it's like an old pair of shoes; sure they're ratty and falling apart but they fit like a glove. The beauty of getting to the root of our core wounds is that once we're consciously aware of a pattern we have the power to change it. Understanding where it began helps us to dissolve all of the coping mechanisms we've developed along the way, this can be anything from overeating and substance abuse to self-effacing behaviors and unhealthy relationships. We develop these patterns as a means of repeatedly reintroducing the issue until we're able to eventually work through it.

This is the process in a nutshell:

We experience something.
We give that experience a meaning.
We integrate that meaning into the story we're telling.
This then patterns in the people and experiences that will help keep the story going.

We can resolve a pattern by becoming aware of it and then change the meaning we've given to it. We honor our evolutionary process once we adopt the perspective that the difficulties we experience serve as an integral part of the process which allows us to discover our talents and self-awareness, so that we may then use it to empower ourselves to consciously create our life.

Emotional Dwellings

The human mind is designed to be an instrument of survival and so its primary purpose is to interpret its experience and identify any potential danger or stress. It's a problem-solving machine, so if it cannot find any problems in the present moment it will often pull up past instances or project potential future ones. And for some, these negative dwellings are played on a continuous loop. They are intentionally referred to as dwellings because many of us live there in our minds, but being aware of these mechanisms is what allows us to consciously direct them in positive ways.

We can reveal our dwellings with a few simple questions:

What subjects or thoughts do we find ourselves consistently preoccupied with?

What people or situations consistently come to mind?

Which ones affect our emotional state the most?

What can we see about our patterns and the story we're telling based on our answers?

These thoughts and memories are used as a means to reinforce a past issue, which keep the same patterns repeating in different ways in our outer experience. If our primary dwelling is an issue around a failed relationship or financial woes it's likely being used to reinforce feelings of inadequacy or disempowerment. And so we continue patterning in people and situations that reinforce a disempowering narrative until which point we're aware enough of it to change it.

An important thing to remember when dwelling on the ways we've been wronged by others is to understand that we are all doing the best we can with where we're at in life. We all struggle in one way or another and some are more lost than others. Viewing things from this perspective gives us the ability to transmute hurt and anger into understanding and hopefully forgiveness. This frees us from allowing other people's actions to change or determine how we feel about ourselves, which is the primary way we reclaim our power.

When I was about 8 years old, I spent a year living with a family member who rarely fed me and among other things would lock me in the attic in 100° heat. Unconsciously I let these experiences create feelings of being unloved, along with a visceral desire for freedom. I was able to transmute the meaning I'd given to these experiences when I did two things:

First, I experienced it as fully as I remembered it to be. Then I neutralized the emotional charge through observation, seeing the memory as objectively as I would reflect on a dream I had or a movie I saw. This happened more organically once I took on the perspective of seeing the Game of Life as an experience program I entered to have these specific experiences, which I chose because they would propel my evolution both supportively and through contrasts and challenges. This change in perspective is what shifted how I viewed all of my experiences and life in general. The next thing I did was transmute the emotion I had tied to it, and I purposely phrase it that way because we tie ourselves to our past through the emotions we associate with it and it's our emotion that sustains these tethers. Like umbilical cords we send our attention and energy to it and it grows as a result. We can also use this process positively by projecting into the future the things we want to experience and then sustaining the tether with powerful positive emotions. This is how we tie ourselves to those things and done with enough potency and alignment we will merge with it.

Initially I had a lot of anger around my past because in my core I believe all people are entitled to love and care, especially children. Once I anchored into a state of awareness rather than the story that was being told about the experience, I was able to enter these experiences as you would a virtual reality. I started having compassion for the person who caused these challenges because as difficult as that time was, it was a far more difficult path to have to live out life as that person, so profoundly lost in their own struggles.

Once we're able to understand that we select our experiences in one way or another, we reclaim our power and are no longer the victim of our experiences or the actions of others. I understand that there are some things that we may never be willing to consider choosing to experience but at the very least we must accept that the awful, even unthinkable things that happened to us have served us in some way. If only for the purpose of breaking our heart open or proving how remarkably resilient we are.

Attractiveness

In this physical experience of ours there are many things we desire to be and have and one of those things to be is attractive. True attractiveness has very little to do with physical appearance, it is the energetic emanation of self-acceptance. Authentic people who are completely comfortable with themselves and accept others as they are are attractive regardless of what they look like. Authenticity is a palpable quality that people naturally gravitate towards and is one of the most significant factors in what makes someone truly attractive, giving them the innate ability to draw others to them with their emanating magnetism.

The key to any truly exceptional person is a vibrant personality. Beauty is entirely relative, while the quality of being attractive is a universal phenomenon; it's the magnetic radiance of oneself, and it's attractive regardless of how it's packaged.

The world responds to how we feel about ourselves and it's designed to give us what we believe we deserve. Once we're able to raise our emanation and the quality of our expectations, we will come to realize the things that we desire. Our results are proportionate to the degree of certainty we have that what we desire will be ours, that in fact it already is, and so much so we can taste it. But so many people don't allow themselves to want something whole heartedly because they can't risk failing at something that truly matters to them. I don't believe in failure but if I did the only real failure is not going for it.

Self-Connection

I've moved enough times in my life to know that making friends is an art form, by the time I'd reached high school I had been to eighteen different schools. I quickly learned to use humor to make friends but even with a well tuned repertoire I still at times would find myself profoundly lonely. This loneliness stretched into adulthood and lasted until I realized how much I enjoy my own company. An integral part of lifelong happiness only comes once we truly enjoy our own company, but with the tech laden life we lead it's rare we experience time with ourselves anymore, let alone enjoy it.

In order to reconnect with myself I started doing things alone, going for meals alone, stop in somewhere for a beverage, go for walks, watch the sunset, take a class, people watch. I guess what I'm trying to say is that I started dating myself and we fell in love. We often lose ourselves in the roles we play; being a professional, a partner and a parent, there's often little of ourselves left over when the day is done. I know doing things alone can sound awful and uncomfortable at first, but every area of life will benefit as a result.

When we accept and connect deeply with ourselves we greatly expand our ability to show up for the other people in our lives, we also start to attract others who are on a similar wavelength. When we are anchored into the wholeness of who we are, we welcome others to live as authentic expressions of who they are which is fertile ground for deep and genuine connections.

The keys to self-empowerment are self-acceptance, authenticity and passion. Quite simply to be ourself and do what we love, and if we don't know what we love then we should start vigorously exploring the things we're drawn to until it eventually reveals itself to us.

Bridging the Gap

The most effective way to bridge where we are to where we want to be is to act as if it already is. Personally I struggled with this crucial principle because it too viscerally pointed out the stark contrast between where I wanted to be and where I was. Fortunately I now understand faking it till you make it much differently than before and this is my understanding: The perspective we think from determines the choices we make and the results and opportunities we receive. Every action brings a result relative to the perspective in which it is being acted from.

Meaning if we're looking for a place to live, a mate, or a job and that choice is coming from the subconscious perspective that we'll take what we can get; the results are going to correspond to the position we're acting from. We could also engage from the higher perspective of only entertaining options that resonate with us because the choice will constitute a good portion of our life and satisfaction. The act of seeking something is the same but the position it is being acted from is entirely different and will carry us down a path that corresponds to the perspective behind the decision: survival or fulfilment.

The key to doing this correctly is imagining the greatest version of our self at our highest apex of achievement. This version could be seated at the head of the boardroom table of a Fortune 500 company, or at the head of the dinner table of a very happy family, or in the director's chair on a blockbuster movie set. Whatever it is, we need to discover our seat of power which belongs to this version of us who has already attained the highest possible success in the area that calls to our heart.

Create a brief and vivid scene observing this version and explore what it *feels* like to be them, to be at this level of mastery and Creatorship. A few times a day, especially upon waking and prior to going to sleep it's remarkably beneficial to anchor into this place of power, if only for a moment, so we may connect to knowing the self-empowerment that comes with fulfilling our potential. Feel what it's like to be this higher version, dropping into this version in the same way an actor slips into a role. Whenever we need to make an important decision in our life, we'll find it remarkably helpful to put ourselves in this higher perspective because it's not so much the decision that matters as much as the perspective the decisions are being made from. It is important to understand that people of power and awareness act from a much more centered place, and once we firmly anchor ourselves at the center of our experience everything around us will begin to shift to reflect the new position we are now playing from.

In the same way, our beliefs are not nearly as important as the actions we take based on what we believe. Most of us cut ourselves off from the life we deserve for no other reason than we're quick to settle for much less. Then later we come to realize that an option wasn't a good fit and for that whole time we were preventing all of the more suitable options from reaching us. We limit ourselves so greatly by choosing low level options and for no other reason than we convince ourselves that it's the best option available and that something's better than nothing. I've made enough decisions in my life to know that a lot of the time nothing is *way* better.

Remember whenever an important choice presents itself to connect to this higher version of ourselves in their seat of power and see what they would do in a given situation, and if it resonates with us then we have our answer. What this does is changes our reference point, by outsourcing it to our higher version we are effectively shifting the level in which we think and operate from and this natural and organic process will put us into alignment with becoming that higher version.

We often think from a very limited reference point. For instance, because it's been a while since the last relationship we've had we choose to accept a partner who is less than ideal for us because we start to doubt if anyone more suitable is going to come along. But what if the very next week we were supposed to meet the person of our dreams only now we're not going to follow the line of events that would have brought us together because we decided to play it safe. When we change our reference point to a higher perspective it opens up a whole different bandwidth of experience and when seated in our power we're much more likely to identify a low-level option for what it is. That's when life becomes a catalogue and we go: "No, that's not really right, what else do you have?" Then more options present themselves and we begin creating this dialogue with our life, which grows more intelligent once we really start to understand what we like and don't like about the options being presented. The more clearly we understand what exactly we're look for the more the field of our experience can refine itself to our preferences and expectations.

The key is to overcome the "I'll take what I can get" survivalist way of being we're indoctrinated with. Even if we have high standards and expectations it's coming from an even higher place when we're anchored into our seat of power. This isn't about ego or perfection, it's about deeply knowing ourselves, understanding what we want and why and having the self-discipline not to settle for anything less, because we only get in life what we're willing to settle for.

The quickest way to raise the quality of the life we're living is to start making decisions from our place of power.

What would they have for lunch?

What would they wear?

What would they be thinking about right now?

How would they handle that challenge?

If they had to live our life for one day how would they do it?

See them doing the things we do every day in their own way and gradually merge with that way of being now. This is the most effective way to bridge the gap from where we are to where we want to be. Only once we become that version will we merge with that version's life, as the two are inextricably bonded together. True progress comes once we realize that our higher version is really just a more joyful and loving version of ourselves, and to become this version we must fill our life with the simple things that help connect us to feeling more joy and love.

External Feedback

Our external world has a powerful effect on our expectations, emotions, mindset and our overall state of being. Any changes we make to our living environment are an outer representation of the inner shift we are making, so we must make them big and noticeable.

Nothing changes if nothing changes.

We can paint our place a different color, move the furniture around, put out pictures, books and other things that reinforce our higher version. These visual cues will help reinforce the shift we're making. Next, clear out the clutter. In the Game of Life, clutter is just vibrational noise, so get rid of it. Keeping our space tidy and organized is a simple yet powerful way to raise our subconscious standards to a higher quality.

Our outer world is a representation of our inner world which is why it's imperative to purge our old version from our life: clean out the closets, the drawers, our phone, emails, our social media, all of it. We must purge everything that represents or reinforces the old version of our life: This could be friends, content, keepsakes, clothes, pictures, journals. Whatever it is, get rid of it. Set a standard and stick to it. Purge everything we're not bringing with us to this new version of our life, then once we've made space we can bring in things that help to reinforce this higher version.

Find ways to incorporate these methods everywhere: In the car, at work, on the screen of our phone, etc. It's important to have things that we'll see often to help reinforce the shift we're making. When we wake up tomorrow it's likely that we could be sleepwalking in the default character and these external cues are a helpful way to wake us up and remind us. The most challenging part of this can be in the beginning when we're playing the new character version in what appears to be the old version's life, but as long as we hold fast and stay consistent, we'll be amazed at how fast things will change around us. And reinforcing that change in our surroundings really helps to accelerate the process.

Since a substantial portion of our lives is spent online it's incredibly important to completely overhaul our social media content: what we're posting, who we're following and interacting with and most importantly to flood our feeds with content that represents our goals and ideals. Start creating boards on Pinterest, this may sound trivial but it's a remarkably simple and effective way to help better understand our interests, tune our resonance, refine our goals, and understand exactly what we're looking to call into our lives. Once we saturate our minds with the things we resonate with they will begin to express themselves in our experience. And for those who are still trying to figure out what this means for them this is a powerful tool to discover the things they are drawn to and enjoy.

In our living space we can reinforce this process by introducing a few items that encapsulate our higher version and placing them where they'll be seen often. The key is to saturate ourselves with this new way of being so that it's constantly reflecting our ideals back to us. For instance, someone who has decided to go for their dream of being a professional boxer could frame pictures of whomever their hero is and put up some quotes to help them get into their mindset. If it were me, I'd find a picture of a championship belt and blow it up to life-size and frame it on my wall so in the corner of my eye my subconscious is picking up that I'm already a champion, and all the effort I'm putting in is just to merge that experience with this one. If you truly believe you are capable of being a champion you will live and prepare like a champion and done with fervent consistency you will become what you persist that you are.

This is true for anything we dream of.

What we're really doing here is setting the stage for the version we're becoming, and our surroundings should imply that we are already at that level, or at least well on our way to becoming it. When we ensure our visual field is constantly reflecting our goals and ideals back to us, it's both a motivation and reminder that this is the standard we've set; the level we've chosen to play the game at, while also familiarizing ourselves with examples of the people we respect who've done it as well.

It's all too easy to get sidetracked by life and designing our space well can keep our head in the game so we can remain focused on achieving our goal. We are fortunate to live in an age of information, making it easier than ever for us to find others who've achieved the epitome of success in what we're trying to do and then saturate ourselves with that content: watch interviews, clips, read or listen to whatever we can find, this will help us to understand the process and embody the necessary mindset. If we haven't yet figured out what our goal is then we can immerse ourselves in the high-level content that interests us and go from there.

Shifting Your Reality

Step 1: Choose a Version

Our higher version is meant to be the highest most ideal version of ourselves that we can conceive of. Some of us know exactly who the higher version is, those who don't know can discover it by figuring out the things they're interested in and really love to do. When was the last time you truly felt excited about something, and what was it? We often dismiss the things we're truly passionate about because at some point we're taught to abandon our dreams and be practical. We can be practical in the way we develop a plan and are systematic in following our dreams, but we must never make ourselves small to fit into the box of what other people think is possible. I don't believe in rules but if there was a rule, Rule #1 would be to follow your excitement. Do what you love, fill your life with it, eat-sleep-and-breathe it.

That is how we build a happy and fulfilling life.

We are all going to encounter challenges in life no matter how practical we're being, so we might as well choose to follow our dreams and do whatever it is we're most passionate about, something that sustains us enough that we'll be able to put in all of the effort and energy necessary to truly succeed at it.

Step 2:
Crafting our External World

This is where we design our surroundings to reinforce our higher version through supportive content, visual cues and motivation. If we don't know who our higher version is then we must first figure out what we love and want to achieve.

The example of the professional boxer could be tailored for any possible field, if someone wanted to be a professional chef, they could print and frame the Michelan star award they give to the best restaurants in the world and hang it where they'll see it while they're cooking. Things like this can be done for absolutely every field and it's such positive and effective feedback.

Step 3:
Establish a Primary Goal

Once we're able to determine our primary goal then we determine the actions necessary to prepare to see it realized. Keeping with the Chef example, my biggest goal would be to open a Michelan star restaurant. I would need stepping stones in order to bridge the gap from where I am to where I want to be. My Pinterest boards would be full of Michelan restaurants, recipes, design photos, menu examples, etc. All of my content would reflect it. Our feedback is our world, so this is how we live in the world we want to right now.

I would set some incremental goals: I would take culinary classes, host dinner parties to try out my recipes, cater dinner parties for others, then pop-up dining experiences and so on until I opened my own place. Goals require incremental action in order to prepare ourselves and our life for what we are looking to call forth. It's our preparation that put us into alignment and allows life to deliver to us all of the auspicious happenings that will carry us further towards realizing our goals.

A friend of mine, the inspiration for the Chef example, fully committed to this process. Even having taken all of the above mentioned steps, she still had no foreseeable way of finding the funding she needed to open her restaurant. But she didn't let a little thing like that stop her— she was adamant on realizing her dream and so she got a commercial agent and began looking at spaces. After seeing about two dozen places, she found the perfect one. She had the agent tell the owners she wanted the space and asked them to meet with her to discuss the terms of the lease. She met with the couple a few days later and brought with her a bevy of tasting spoons so they could sample all of her best dishes. As they ate, she explained her vision for the space and asked them to hold it for her for the next six weeks while she finished securing the funding she needed. Impressed by her passion and culinary prowess they agreed, and she went off to summon a miracle. Despite doing everything she could think of, at the end of the six weeks she had the agent inform the owners that she would not be taking it. About a week later she received a call from them and with it an offer to invest in the restaurant. And three years later she received her Michelin Star.

If you provide the passion and preparation, the world will deliver to you everything else.

"Luck is what happens when preparation meets opportunity."

For some people the shift to a higher version is exactly the answer they've been looking for and so their change is complete and immediate, they definitively shed the old one and fully commit to the new one and there's no looking back. For others the process is more transitional like moving into a new house one box at a time.

Step 4:
Develop a Higher Routine

In the beginning the old version may stick around initially and this is because it's currently set as our default player, so every day we're going to have to consciously select the new player when we wake up. This is why making changes to our surroundings is so important in anchoring in the new, having powerful visual cues that we see when we wake up is very helpful in making the transition.

Another way to anchor in the change we're making is to create a daily routine based on what we imagined our highest version doing when they were living a day in our life. And if at any point we find ourselves dwelling on the narrative of the old character version we must immediately withdraw our attention, affirm that's the old character and consciously select the new one; reminding ourselves of the higher version we're choosing to be and why it's a better choice.

It can feel like a daunting task to try to become something new but all we really need is to do it for one day. If we master one day, through repetition we can master our whole life. Do it for one day and the next day will be better as a result. There is such powerful momentum in habit, we just need to sustain the effort for the time it takes to anchor in the habit and then the momentum will help to carry us the rest of the way.

The Inner Game

Our internal world is the hidden game board in the Game of Life, the primary plane where all of our personal evolution takes place. There came a great shift in my life the moment I decided to lean into the madness instead of using all my effort and energy to try to hide, avoid or change it. On some level we are all broken, crazy and odd. Yes, there are varying degrees, but it's been proven that the more of those three we have (when properly cultivated) have the potential to make us a genius in our field.

If we pop the hood of our inner being and take a look at the mess, all of the idiosyncrasies, trauma and self-sabotage and we say: "You know what— I accept this ghastly heap." Knowing that in all of the unsightliness there lies our superpower and that is our ability to be authentic, to be fully and unapologetically the person we came here to be. People want to be liked but what people really like is what's open, honest and genuine and the irony is that a lot of the time those are the very things we're not bringing to our interactions and experiences.

I always find it interesting to observe all of the different versions people shift into depending on who they're interacting with. When someone slips into parent mode, employee mode, any of the countless modes and roles we play throughout the day. Each role we play comes with its own autopiloted mode of behavior, tone, posture, language and experience, and every mode we run keeps us asleep. This continues until which point we start to bring a deep sense of ourselves to our interactions.

The mechanics of our inner interface works like this: We experience something and that neutral stimulus then travels through the many filters of our perception which molds it into a narrative. I could hand someone a flower, just the neutral act of handing them a flower could prompt one of a litany of different responses. It could prompt a romantic feeling, or a memory of a funeral and make them sad, it could mean nothing, it could be their grandmother's favourite flower and make them feel nostalgic, they could love the color or not like the scent, there are a million different ways it could go. The neutral happening is internalized where it is imbued with a narrative which arouses some spectrum of feeling and relationship to it. The feeling emits a frequency which passes back into the external world and affects the way the rest of the experience unfolds.

Anchoring Points

An anchoring point is some form of feedback that we use as a trigger to become more aware or to reinforce a habit or belief. The power of anchoring points can be used in a few different ways. They can be used to create an external reminder to return to a state of awareness, to pivot or transform a trigger into an opportunity to reprogram how we engage, and to reinforce a new positive narrative or belief. There are people who use internal cues like dwelling as reminders to center themselves and affirm something positive, while others use external cues as a way to reinforce a higher narrative that will help them create a much happier and more fulfilling life.

Here's an example: I have a friend who loves the number 7 and considers it to be very lucky. It was suggested to him that every time he would see 7,77,777, to get excited and in this state of excitement to affirm how lucky he is. Over the span of a few months he worked himself into a white heat about how lucky he is. Affirming how lucky he was all the time greatly improved his happiness and satisfaction in daily life for no other reason than he had changed his perception to celebrate what he already had and so he kept being given reasons to keep his narrative going. Through this process he also managed to transform an unfruitful interest in gambling into a lucrative income. His skill had in no way improved during that period, what shifted was his now electric belief that he was lucky and so the field of experience delivered to him the things that would support the story he was telling, and with each success he had it fed his belief like rocket fuel.

The remarkable thing is we can do this with absolutely any cue or belief, but the key is to use something that elicits a positive reaction in us. The more powerfully it creates a response the more it will help to anchor us into realizing what we desire. It is my hope that the sign on the cover of this book and the barcode on its back will act as anchoring points for you and that any time you see either cue in daily life you allow it to return you to a state of wakefulness and awareness of the game you're playing. It is also helpful to pick other things that stand out to you personally, as visual reminders to return to the fullness of your experience and also to help you to reinforce the story you wish to tell about your life.

Bio-Reality

The inner world we live in can be looked upon as our bio-reality. Here we will explore how our bio-reality is created, the information contained in this section is meant to give people the power to transcend negative bio-feedback loops like anxiety and depression and cultivate a more ideal internal reality.

Our consistent emotional states become our bio-reality, the internal world of experience on a chemical level. How bio-reality works is simple. Our thoughts, actions and bio-baselines cause a release of biochemicals either positive or negative, which are interpreted by the body as emotions and prompt more thoughts related to that feeling. This creates a loop which generally repeats itself until the loop has built up a great deal of momentum. We all have experienced this on both the positive and negative spectrums, each of which has an equal and distinct momentum.

The more momentum a positive loop has the more expansive it feels, while the more momentum a negative loop has the tighter and more constrictive it feels. Depression and anxiety are just the result of a negative bio-feedback loop that consistently repeated itself until it formed a negative baseline.

So how do we change it?

People experience negative feedback loops for four main reasons: unresolved trauma, dwelling on the past, being dissatisfied with current circumstances, and projecting or imagining negativity in the future, often it's a combination of all of them. The reason why feeling this way leaves us so depleted is because all of the negative biochemistry this releases draws on our vital life force. We often think of positive and negative as good and bad but what negative really is is subtractive it reduces while positive is additive, it increases. So in the equation of emotions if we're consistently in a negative bio-loop, our emotional accounts are over-drawn and the only way to balance the books is by introducing some positive dividends.

It's been known that if we hold a thought for seventeen seconds one just like it will join it (and another and another) until that thought has fused with its correlating emotion and has a momentum all its own, and this is true for both positive and negative cycles. The harder we feel it's going to be to change the loop the more likely it's because it has woven itself into our conception of who we are now. It's become so embedded that we start to believe that it's just the way it is and it can't be changed.

The bottom line is that when we feel like something's just happening to us we're at the mercy of it and don't have any power to change it. But understanding how these things work is what allows us to reclaim the power we have to direct our lives and determine the quality of our experience through consciously choosing how we direct our attention in both our inner and outer world.

We always have the power to determine our bio-reality, this includes both how we think and how we feel. There are times that our minds are like runaway horses and these negative thoughts and emotions just loop without us realizing all of the negative biochemistry it's spurting out. This emotional momentum can only be sustained with more thoughts that help to perpetuate and amplify the emotion, and this is true for both the positive and negative loops. But power comes in realizing that these loops have to be fed in order to keep their momentum.

It's the mind's job to identify the negatives in our external world as a means of survival and if it can't find any immediate threats it will often dig some up. So if we don't give the mind direction it will pick one for us and it's usually a negative one. If we don't have something positive to pour our energy into our minds will conjure something to consume that energy in another away. We are energy generating beings so if we don't find productive ways to expend and invest our energy, we will unconsciously develop tactics that expend it in other ways.

Our Bio-Reality works like this:

We have a thought which prompts an emotion and that emotion prompts more of those kinds of thoughts which perpetuates and amplifies that physiological state. A loop is created and the longer it's run the greater the momentum and emotional charge it will have, and this is true for both the negative and positive states.

So how do we change a loop we're in?

The key is recognizing a negative thought before the seventeen seconds, at which point it gains momentum. The reason some people feel like they don't have the power to shift their negative into a positive is because their default loop has been persistently negative. If that's the case, then there's a simple way of interrupting the loop through a positive change in our physiology which immediately bypasses the brain and tells the body we're calm or happy. This is done through breathing and the way we're holding our body. If we're not too far gone smiling, chuckling or even jumping-jacks are effective ways of interrupting the bio-feedback loop. What I personally do is take a conscious breath and internally remind myself that I am the awareness behind the thought or experience I'm having. This helps to return me to a state of neutrality so I may better understand the story or relationship I have to whatever caused me to enter that loop.

In addition to conscious breathing, there are other lifestyle factors necessary to ensuring a positive bio-feedback loop: being active, eating well, getting sunlight and fresh air, abstaining from drugs and alcohol, limiting sugar intake, getting enough sleep, consuming positive material, and surrounding ourselves with supportive people. Going for a walk is such a powerful tool for shifting our emotional state and so is listening to some uplifting music, drinking a glass of water or taking a quick rinse in the shower.

Many people think that their thoughts are the most important part of the equation but it's not, emotion is. This is because there are two types of thought, objective thought which are thoughts that have no emotion and are usually functional in nature; like mentally rehearsing the day, thinking about what we're going to have for lunch, etc. These are relatively devoid of emotion and so they possess no power or magnetism. The second type is subjective thought, which are any thoughts imbued with emotion, the power and magnetism they contain is directly proportionate to the amount of emotion they have behind them.

Emotion is energy in motion and the more emotion a thought contains the more powerfully it is projected into the quantum field through the electromagnetism it generates. Many people learn this and then obsess about the quality of their thoughts, which often degrades into a sort of toxic positivity. We set out to have only positive thoughts and then we worry, and then we worry that we're worrying, and so on.

Emotion supersedes thought because it creates a chemical reaction in the body, that not only radiates outward electromagnetically but also prompts more thoughts and feelings relative to that chemical state. Cortisol, adrenalin, serotonin and oxytocin will elicit the thoughts and feelings we've wired to them. Each of us has developed

our own ways to release these chemicals on command which are usually done habitually and often in ways that can deplete us.
We all have bio-chemical baselines and we crave the chemistry that our body's used to. Our body and mind want what it's used to even if it's uncomfortable because what it knows is much more comfortable than the unknown. For many people their physical systems are used to high levels of the stress hormone cortisol, this often creates a pattern of obsessive thinking and worrying in order to provide the constant mental stimulus necessary to maintain the steady stream of cortisol that their body is used to.

After this process reaches its peak, it's usually followed by a coping mechanism adopted to provide relief through release of the body's pleasure and reward chemicals. This is often achieved through eating, drinking, shopping, sex, gaming, TV, social media bingeing, etc. These pleasure rewards are short-lived and often need to be done continuously to get the effects we crave.

So how do we effectively alter our body chemistry?

The simplest answer is: Breathing.

Breathing is the number one way to instantly affect our biochemistry. Right now just take a nice comfortable deep breath. All it takes is one conscious breath and our body begins releasing beneficial biochemistry. Even awareness sets in for as long as we can maintain it.

There are two reasons why our biochemistry determines the type of thoughts we have. The first is that the chemical state of our body determines the brainwave state or our mind which determines how the brain operates. Stress often causes High Beta brainwaves, which are generally very erratic, like a neural lightening storm. While the relaxed and meditative states of Alpha and Theta are coherent and calm. Breath and mindfulness are the simplest ways to transform both brainwaves and biochemistry. Yawning can be another unexpected way to shift our brainwave state.

The second reason why our biochemistry determines our thoughts is because we've wired each bio-chemical state to associate with specific types of thoughts, feelings and activities. Through repetition we create default loops of thinking, feeling and doing which build up a lot of momentum. It's important to remember that these processes are incredibly beneficial once they're geared towards the positive.

True Reality

There are layers to reality on both the collective and individual levels, and at the very core of all reality lies the ultimate reality, which one can only enter through the heart. This is the kingdom referred to in biblical allegory available to those who "become like little children" i.e. live from the heart.

This version of reality is revealed to us once the perceptive filters of the mind are peeled back so the vividness of the true reality may reveal itself. True in the sense that it is pure, free from subjectivity, being just as it is. As we begin to free ourselves of the default urge the mind has to enforce our will and analysis upon our external world, we become more accepting, present and engaged with our experiences and are able to perceive the magic of existence just as it is. This refines our ability to see beauty in the most seemingly ordinary things which brings with it a great joy, depth and connection.

So how does one experience the True Reality?

We have experienced the true reality anytime we've connected with our experience in a way that feels like we are one with it. Any moment where we feel that we are in complete union with our outer experience, that we are just an interwoven expression of each other.

All that we encounter in our personal reality is merely an extension of the frequency we are emanating, and transcendence is any direct experience of this fundamental truth. As we continue to clarify our being and release the programming and perceptive filters we've inherited and developed, we begin to realize ourselves as the clear conduits for the divine flow of creation. And in doing so we find union with the nourishing beauty and magnificence of this moment which can, if we let it, stretch out to occupy our whole life.

So how does one be a clear conduit for the Flow?

The less we carry the debris of who we think we are with us into the moment, the more powerfully we can connect with it and become a unified expression. The greats are great because they have the ability to shed themselves and merge with the creative flow that propels life to unfold. Most of us carry so many preconceptions, patterns, motivations and desires with us through life and each thing acts as a filter that the flow has to pass through before it finally reaches us, and by the time it does it's stripped of its essence and all that remains is a highly skewed mental conception.

Presence and flow are about dropping the firewall of the mind and the constructs of the ego and just directly experiencing something, almost as if through osmosis or diffusion; allowing it to permeate our being. This is the truest form of connection one can possibly have, allowing ourselves to merge with the experience we are having.

Realm of The Ultimate

As previously mentioned, I have had the benefit of experiencing a few plant medicine ceremonies and every ceremony regardless of the medicine behind the journey allows me to arrive at the same place. It's *Here* with a capital H. The divine version of reality that is woven into all of creation and available to us in every moment. Though my initial contact was facilitated with entheogens, I now naturally connect to Here on a regular basis. It's paradoxical to arrive here, yet also always be here, or at least always have the potential to be here in every moment. What I refer to as Here is called many things: The Eternal Now, The Kingdom, Flow, The 5D, A New Earth, etc.

Here is the greatest place one could be, where we feel radiant, in our essence and supremely connected to the moment and those around us. It's a blissful paradise where we find peaceful reverence in the realization that everything is perfect just as it is.

The irony is that we always have the ability to be Here, we're just too busy trying to get *there* to realize it. Life is spent living in our heads instead of inhabiting the moment, let alone allowing it to inhabit us. Here is the greatest place one could be, and can be accessed whenever we are in a state of energetic alignment. When operating in a state of alignment we feel electric, beaming, and profoundly nourished by a supreme feeling of connection.

Imagine creation as a great cosmic geyser of lifeforce energy. When we are fully centered, we come into alignment with this wellspring of cosmic essence which lights up our internal spectrum. This spectral alignment unlocks the higher modes of perception which grant us access to this ultimate version of reality. The only way to anchor into this alignment is through heart perception, receiving our experience from the level of our being rather than the mind. The veils to the higher realms are thinner than ever which has given a great many of us the opportunity to access this ultimate version of reality.

So how does one get Here?

The directions are simple: Be Here Now.

This is not just some new age catchphrase; it's the coordinates to the ultimate realm of experience. Once we center ourselves in the heart we can use these coordinates to reveal a higher realm of experience.

>Be — Tap into is the fullness of your being,
>the infinite awareness behind the experience.
>
>Here — Tap into the fullness of your sensory experience, just as it is.
>
>Now — Tap into the omnificent centerpoint of the moment that is forever unfolding.

Some may wonder if Here and Now are the same thing; they are the experiential expressions of both space and time and the fundamental axis upon which our physical reality is built.

Whenever I am fully Here, I'm beaming, carried forward effortlessly by an uplifting and synchronistic flow from beginning to end. I am perpetually impressed by the beauty and intelligence of the interface, its symbiotic nature with our inner being and its reflection in our outer world. Our reality is an endless feedback system, reflecting the quality of our emanation back to us in plain sight. It's just that most of us are too submerged in the mind to take notice of its ever-present subtlety.

The paradox is that it's always here, yet we also need to find our way home to it. This is much more about the internal journey from the head to the heart than anything else. How easily we can connect to the ultimate realm is determined almost entirely by how readily we can exit the world of our mind.

Here is perfect just as it is. It's pure flow and there's no striving to do or to have, just to experience the fullness of what is before us. Falling in love is the quickest way to ensure that we may experience the fullness of Here. We're floating, the sun shines brighter, everything tastes better, even the air is sweeter. This is because our heart is so activated that it becomes our primary center of perception, until the mind takes over again.

Anytime we've found ourselves admiring how truly perfect something is, we've been Here. Anytime we've been mesmerized by the intangible beauty, vividness or the surreal feeling of something, we've been Here. Anytime we've been lit up by our own essence and self-expression, we've been Here.

Others have referred to this deeper realm of experience as Paradise or Heaven on Earth but it's just Here. It's the perfect name for it; obvious yet subtle, unremarkable yet profound. We will never be any place but here, yet we often miss it entirely trying to get there.

Here and Now is the axis upon which the Game of Life is designed, it is experiential expression of space and time and the craziest thing is that our brains filter out this ultimate reality by default. The last place the brain wants to be is Here, here is when all striving ends and isness reigns supreme and that gives the brain *nothing* to grasp at, so it gets uncomfortable and avoids the here and now at all costs. The mind chooses instead to operate on the axis that constrictive illusion is built upon; There and Then. This is the ultimate dupe, because there is no there or then, it can and will only ever be here and now. Yet we spend all of our time and energy trying to get there and in doing so we miss the treasure that is subtly all around us. The magic and beauty of this higher realm is so subtle and ephemeral that it's easy to miss it entirely, the key is to understand that we must tune ourselves to the perception of it.

Anytime we feel truly connected to ourselves, others and our experience, we are Here. So the task then becomes to fill our life with the things that make us feel this way now. Fully engaging with our experience is the primary prerequisite for experiencing this higher reality. At first we often just glimpse Here, like a surfer catching a brief and exhilarating wave.

So what exactly is Here?

This goes far beyond mere presence in daily life. Here is the ultimate reality where life feels like a supremely vivid and lucid dream. Being able to access this higher realm of experience all comes down to being able to hold the elevated frequencies necessary. Our stamina is continually improving as we are able to hold higher frequencies for longer periods. Look upon it like this: We humans are all made as standard 60-watt lightbulbs and the divine reality of Here runs at 100 watts, it's possible to increase our wattage capacity from 60 to 100 but this has to be done gradually so that it doesn't blow the fuse. So our frequency is gradually increased and these energetic increases are what dissolve the veils of ordinary perception so that the higher realms may be experienced.

Whenever we come across others while in this higher realm of being, we discover that all of the individuals we encounter are just wonderful good-hearted people. We will find ourselves having authentic interactions and feeling of sense of community and being connected to those around us regardless of whether we are interacting with them.

Now as sublimely perfect as the higher realms are, we do need to return to the ordinary planes to experience polarity so we may grow and find balance and equilibrium. The way the game is currently designed we must return to the lower planes of experience to seek and strive and learn but the higher we ascend the phases and levels of the Game of Life the more we get to claim paradise as our primary residence which has an entirely different set of creative principles associated with it as outlined in the Creatorship and Godship levels.

Climbing the Mountain

The thing we want most in life, the thing that is the most important and illusive to us, is the mountain we will climb. Climbing this mountain will often entail traveling a road of the opposite of what we whole-heartedly desire, which often makes achieving this thing feel monumentally challenging, farfetched, or downright impossible. This is purposefully designed to make reaching the summit taste so sweet. If the mountain just took a leisurely stroll to get to the top, getting to the top wouldn't mean anything. It would be nothing more than a nice view we briefly enjoy. And for this reason, the game is designed to have us traverse the perilous terrain of things that reinforce the opposite of what we desire as we make our way to our unique version of the top. But only the willful and strong of heart will make it to the top of their mountain because it's often takes all that we've got to get there, and it's purposefully designed this way.

Figuring out what mountain we're climbing and what lies at the top of it is an imperative part of understanding our own personal game. We each carry with us a specific goal that is a unique product of who we are as an individual as well as the specific void that has been created by our journey of polarity.

Let's say someone wants to be an A-list director and has honed their skills for decades and as a result they have both the vision and the talent to make them a world class director. They've even tasted some success having award winning films at film festivals, yet they are still faced with a seemingly perpetual Catch-22; that all the big directorial work is reserved for those with big directorial work under their belts. This makes the ultimate goal at the peak of the mountain feel seemingly impenetrable, at least until more favourable weather moves in and the path to the peak becomes clearer. So many of us find ourselves in this B version of the A world we truly want to reach and sometimes there's such a stark contrast between what we desire and what we're actually experiencing that it makes us question if there really is a top this mountain after all, and if there is, do we have what it takes to get there?

The answer is Yes.

This is your mountain, it has specifically been designed for you and the journey you're on. Of course you're meant to reach the summit, that's the whole reason why you started the climb in the first place.

Once we understand that the game is specifically designed in this manner, we can start to anchor into the knowing that we are already that peak version of ourselves now and all we can do in the meanwhile is skillfully navigate the path we encounter as we diligently refine our skills and prepare ourselves for the peak. Doing this ensures that in every moment we are becoming more fully an expression of our highest potential. This is why comparison is so utterly pointless, because we are all climbing entirely different mountains.

At the peak of our mountain is the thing we've deeply yearned to have or experience and often entwined with this is what we'll give to others and the world; our offering, the contribution we will make that is unique to us and the journey we're on. Our climb up the mountain often determines what is at the peak because what we encounter on our journey determines what our heart needs to realize in this lifetime as well as what we desire to bring forth into the world. Each step on the path carries us closer towards the top. It's true that sometimes we appear to get lost and wander off the path entirely but in actuality; it's all path. It is all purposefully designed and all getting lost really is is the part of our journey where we need to forge our own way of traveling up the mountain.

We have chosen this specific mountain we are climbing to show others that it can be summited. Meaning that coded into our path we have chosen to take on certain challenges that the collective continually wrestle with and as we surmount these things we make the path clearer for others navigating the same challenges, just as our ancestors have cleared the way for us.

Many people deeply desire fame to be at their peak, though many won't allow themselves to admit it. The desire for fame is quite natural as it stems from the deep need we have to be acknowledged and valued. On my climb up the mountain, I've encountered a great deal of the opposite of the things I desire for the sole reason that the goal will taste so much sweeter for having known its opposite. The peak wouldn't feel so profound if climbing it was just a leisurely stroll up a bike path, but those who have dangled over jagged cliffs are the ones whose reaching the peak will truly touch their soul. And that is what most of us are quietly yearning for, for something to touch us so deeply it nourishes us in way that nothing else could. We sign up to climb this mountain of ours for the purpose of reaching that "it was all worth it" moment. It's just that a lot people forfeit pursuing the things that would actually make their suffering and struggles truly worth it.

The key to decoding the peak of our mountain is understanding the feeling that lies behind the thing we want most in life. Those who desire fame as their peak goal would benefit from understanding that it's far more about the feeling we receive from the thing we desire, which in fame's case is acknowledgement. The same is true for those who have set fortune at the peak of their mountain, when the feeling they actually desire is a sense of value or accomplishment. At the end of the day we all want to feel like we matter. How we wish that to manifest for us is entirely relative and is certainly worth exploring and understanding. It's only natural that if we spent a good portion of our lives feeling overlooked or disempowered, we would yearn to experience the opposite. The peak of the mountain is our external validation that we matter in the way that means the most to us. It's a testament of our commitment and resiliency and brings with it the joy and satisfaction that comes with finally conquering the mighty mountain we've been climbing all our lives.

The climb gets remarkably easier once we realize that we already are who we want to be at the peak despite any illusions we encounter that might lead us to believe otherwise. And the more we realize that we already contain within us our peak version, the easier it is for us to ascend to realizing our golden goal. The process is much more about revealing than it is becoming. It's about doing things that bring our peak version out in us more. It's already there, it just needs to be evoked continually until it becomes our primary version.

Once we isolate the feeling we're really after the task then becomes to do things that connect us with that feeling now and to fill our life with them. We further ascend the mountain once we understand that we get what we give, quite literally, so if we are acknowledging another or making someone feel valued, we feel it in return which aligns us greatly to reaching our peak and so our path becomes clearer. If you want to receive something, which in essence is really just a feeling, give it to others. If you wish to feel happy, do something to make someone else happy and you will feel it too.

You get what you give.

I try often to acknowledge others with kindness, it could be as simple as a smile, saying thank you, helping someone in need, or holding a door. We are given many opportunities for this everyday but we're often too busy chasing our own peak to take the time to realize these golden opportunities designed into our path. Once I started providing others with what I wanted to receive I ascended towards the peak quicker and easier than ever before. This is a deliberate part of the design because all who reach the peak have a great deal of power and influence, so by discovering our interrelatedness; that we are all just extensions of one another, we become a more empathetic and effective leader in our lives and the world around us. We must be the change that we want to see in the world, that is how we change it. And the beautiful thing is that most often the change is immediate. This is our mountain, our world and the more we act as a thoughtful and finessing force of positive presence the more everything will transform for us and those around us.

We are the mountain we are climbing and those who truly realize this have already summited or are well on their way. The more we start to see the divine magic that lies subtly beneath the surface of creation, the more it will come out and play with us. And the more we honor those we share our path with, the more we will receive that privilege in return. Many people have allowed their struggles to make them stingy with their kindness or passion when in actuality they're really only shortchanging themselves. The only peace and joy we will find at the top of the mountain is however much we bring up with us.

What is waiting for us at the top of the mountain is the thing we've persistently lacked and therefore always dreamed of having. Upon reaching the summit we will then embark on the next phase as we move ever upward in our evolutionary journey.

The Missing Piece

In the world that forms our personal reality there exist specific voids, things that are clearly missing. The things that are obviously absent in our life often point to what lies on the top of the mountain for us; the hard-fought things we will finally receive and experience upon reaching the summit.

The voids we encounter in our world on a personal level are also there to show us what we can bring into the world for others. If our life has been relatively devoid of love, kindness or guidance it's our task to bring those things into the world for others in whatever way resonates with us. For instance, someone who didn't have a supportive childhood could choose to coach or mentor youth in some way. Each of us is quietly tasked to right the wrongs we've experienced, we signed up for those specific challenges for a reason and those who look to rectify the injustices they've known themselves heal both their personal and the collective journey.

There is no such thing as an insignificant act.

On the level of our purpose and goals there will also be things missing in the world that only we seem to see. Often they are quite obvious to us and this is because we are meant to bring those things into the world. For me personally, there are few tech ventures that I still don't understand how after all these years nobody else has created them yet. These things can and will have a monumental impact on the way we live so it amazes me that these voids remain unfulfilled. But it makes sense once we understand that we were specifically designed to see these missing pieces because we contain the ability to bring them forth into the world. Just in the way that Henry Ford was meant to build the automobile and Steve Jobs to build Apple, so too are we designed to bring forth whatever we feel called to.

I am reminded of the saying: "Talent hits a target nobody else can hit. Genius hits a target nobody else can see." If you can see it, maybe that means it's your target. If a void is clear and obvious to us it's likely because we are the one meant to bring it forth. It could be a business, a song, a technology, or even children. Whatever is calling to you, is calling to you because you were likely chosen to bring it into the world. Sometimes it feels like things are calling us in different directions and we just have to gage ourselves and see if our heart's really in it. It might be meant for us to develop at a later phase or for someone else to. If we are meant to do it, we will, that's how it's been designed. If we feel like nothing is calling to us, it's likely because we abandoned our dreams of fulfilling higher possibility and have settled on what is safe and known.

Every person who's achieved monumental things generally had a hell of a time scaling their mountain to do it. The climb's difficultly level is determined by how high we've set our goals. Are we climbing to the top of ski hill? Or are we climbing Everest? The difficulty level we're climbing at determines the glory that awaits us at the top; the higher the peak, the greater the view.

There is often a consistent theme in the Game of Life: The unseen artist, the unheard musician, the unloved lover, the writer whose work remains on the shelf, the superstar stuck being a background extra. It doesn't mean that it's pointless, quite the opposite, to do those things is the whole point; to hold fast to our dreams and continue to prepare ourselves for the moment when we finally get the big break we've waited our whole lives for. We just have to keep the dream alive and trust in the timing. It's up to the rhythms of life to decide when they will bloom and bare the sweetest fruit one could ever taste.

The voids we experience are specifically designed for both character development and to build up our passion and drive. It's the pressure and suffering to realize our dreams which transforms a lukewarm interest, talent or desire into the consuming passion that allows us to refine our ability to contribute something great. We must find comfort and assurance that the things that have eluded us our entire life are the things we will come to realize at the top of the mountain, and above all we must persist long enough to reach them.

The biggest mistake people make in life is the assumption that the way it's been is the way it will always be. Life is specifically designed for us to experience the fullness of polarity, to have the benefit of *both* poles of experience. Every game is designed with the path to win it, it's just many people forfeit the belief that winning is even possible. The key to winning is simple; a clear vision of what winning means to us then not giving up until we see our vision realized. Most of us just don't allow ourselves to admit the thing we really want to do, and truly believe it's possible for us to attain it. How silly— The Hero is always meant to do astonishing things, against all odds. That's what makes them the Hero!

You are the Star: The Hero

Much like the film *The Truman Show*, you are the star of this show you experience as your life. We must come to realize that we are the main character, the Hero of this story that we are living.

The key to having a great show is living a compelling story and being a Hero people can root for. Understanding that our thoughts are the narration of our show, and our actions, intentions and expectations are its plotline. Would people want to watch the show you are living? It doesn't matter if it appears ordinary on the surface, we can make it a good show entirely by the way we're showing up to it, regardless of what's happening on the surface. The human experience is riveting. I have a friend who is incredibly intelligent, truly an elite mind in this world, yet in the new season of his show he suddenly found himself in a menial entry level cubicle job. I met him for coffee in the lobby of a monolithic glass tower in the financial district and we proceeded to catch up. When I asked him how he was doing he motioned that he wanted to blow his brains out. He confided in me he was deeply depressed, because even with a Master's degree from Stanford he somehow found himself in this ridiculous plot twist. I suggested that he carry out his daily life like he was playing a role in a movie and to narrate it with his thoughts. He perked up at the suggestion. I told him to think of it like the beginning of the Matrix or Fight Club when the Hero is trapped in a world they don't belong in and to passionately play the role on own his terms. The glimmer in his eyes sang like trumpets that I got through to him.

My friend not only rose to the occasion, he soared. And in doing so he claimed the role of Hero in his show. He went on living his daily life with new vigor and when the excitement started to wear off, he decided to make a big move. Working as a self-professed minion for one of the big banks, one night when he was brooding over where to take the story, he decided to hack their system as a civilian then emailed the executive in charge pointing out all of their security weak points. Were they upset? Yes. Did they offer him a lucrative salary and a corner office? Also, yes. But he didn't take it, he told them he would fix their system as an independent contractor and now he does this for financial organizations all around the world. My friend had no formal education in computer science, but it was always a passion, the hobby he would fill his nights with. And so he blazed his own trail and in doing so he rightfully attained his Hero status.

The point is he could have gave into the despair of a bleak circumstance and forfeited the game because he believed he couldn't win, a lot of people do, but he didn't and so he transmuted it from a block to a spring board and used it to propel himself to the top of the mountain. What happens in life is actually of very little significance, all of the power lies in how we respond to what happens, this true for all games. There is always that point in the show or movie when the Hero is just about to realize victory then something arises between them and their goal, and this can happen repeatedly. The key to success is realizing that these are not signs of failure but rather signs that we are getting closer to realizing what we desire. This perspective takes some practice, but it makes all the difference.

We must play the role we've been given and play it in a way that takes to us the top of the mountain. This is the role of a lifetime, the role we were literally designed to play. Play it well, with heart and authenticity. If we are able to connect with the depth of human experience in our personal journey it will be a great story. The grand story we are telling is just the story of going from where we are now to where we know in our heart this story is going. We can make it a compelling show by playing our role in a way that makes it visceral and real, to pour our heart into it. This is what makes someone a Hero we all can root for.

Most people spend a good portion of their lives trying to break through, to be in a position where they feel like they have the power to create their experience and fulfill their potential. We have the power to do that only once we realize that we are constantly creating our experience through our relationship to it, which is just our interpretation of what it means for us. Our life is really nothing more than the story we're telling about it and if we want a new story we have to tell a new one. Most people keep telling the same story, desperately hoping that a new one will finally present itself. The story we are telling is the life we are going to live. It's as simple as that. If you want a new story, you have to tell a new story and this takes commitment and effort.

All success requires a proportional level of delusional self-belief; an utter denying of the surface of our experience coupled with a knowing of what's really happening beyond the illusion of what we encounter. We use the experiences of our life, both positive and negative to reinforce who we are in one way or another and if we can consciously cultivate this process, then we have discovered the keys to creating our life. We will find that as we persist in our higher narrative despite the illusion of our circumstance, our outer world will transform to align with the story we are telling. This will start as little synchronistic signs in the field of our experience which we should use to anchor more fully into the knowing that the internal story we are telling is now revealing itself externally. This will evolve in exponential ways until we come to find ourselves at the point where we've finally realized the storyline we have been telling so diligently. It's our commitment to the story we're telling and by extension the character we're playing that determines our results.

These are not just theories, this is the roadmap used by every person who has ever achieved something, especially something monumental. The biggest leap of my life came when I started using my external world to reinforce my goal. I would somehow relate what was happening to be a part of achieving what I wanted. I would use it as confirmation that everything I wanted to realize was coming into being. And if it was too challenging of an experience to do that then I would just see it for what it is; a stark contrast meant to be a compelling plot point that will make victory taste even sweeter.

Reaching our version of the top often requires us to play a role on the surface while deeply denying to accept anything but the fulfillment of what we desire. We often must pay lip-service to the surface of our reality, while deeply knowing what's going on behind the scenes. We must anchor ourselves firmly in the knowing that we already are who we want to be and already have all that we want, while simultaneously making a great deal of effort to prepare ourselves to step into that role when it presents itself. If we can possess the fortitude to commit to this completely, the veil of illusion will fall away and reveal the prize we knew was ours all along.

The Game of Life is designed for us to realize that the limitation of our circumstance is an illusion we are meant to transcend. Through this understanding we can get the field of our experience to bend to our will and produce what we desire. The paradox is that it requires both an iron will and also full acceptance of what is presented to us each step of the way. We must not resist the process but rather skillfully work with it as it is all specifically designed to aid us in our development and the realization of our goals; understanding that if something is happening it is serving us in some way. All power lies in our response as we play our role from the highest possible perspective. That is how we really play the game, but it takes a great deal of commitment and will to do that. Passion helps make the process a little more effortless but it still requires a considerable amount of heart and persistence.

At this level of the game it's no longer about believing, it's about knowing. It's about having our goal become an internally irrefutable fact, an extension of who we are. We are telling this story, and then things arise to keep that story going. We will only ever experience a continuation of the story we are telling, so being aware of our narrative is the key to discovering the power we have to form a new one. Think of the universal field as entering each of our thoughts, feelings and actions into the cosmic computer which act as direct commands to the field of our experience. This is the real system we are trying to transcend. The programming matrix does not need to be escaped from, it needs to be commandeered, and we do this by consciously cultivating the story we are telling about our life.

So many people want a new story, but it takes diligent self-awareness to consciously form a new narrative and this often requires a constant skewing of every circumstance and experience to mentally conform to the new story we're telling in some way. It takes an unrelenting commitment to tell the new story and only the new story; reframing everything that comes our way until it naturally begins to adapt to the narrative we are telling. If done with enough consistency and knowing, it will be realized. Every one of us is writing, directing and starring in the story we are telling of our life and only the ones who commandeer the creative process and consciously cultivate their narrative will come to realize the life they dream of.

The Edge of Reality

At the very edge of the life we are living there lies a mystical veil and on the other side of that veil is the ideal life we deserve to experience. It is always very clear when we've reached the edge of our reality. It requires courage, persistence and the discomfort that comes with living for a period in a perpetual state of uncertainty as we navigate life on the edge. It may feel like there's no path in front of us and that the old world behind us is disintegrating, but it's supposed to. As we find the resiliency to continue to put one foot in front of the other the veil dissolves and the path appears, revealing the way to realizing our greatest dreams.

Fortune favors the brave and that's because it takes a lot of courage to live life on the edge of the unknown, and that is the only way to make a quantum leap. For those unfamiliar with the quantum physics term it is referring to the remarkable ability particles have to leap from A to Z without having to cover any of the points in between. Since we too are governed by the same universal laws, these astounding shifts are also available to us but it requires an unanchored period of surrender to the instability and uncertainty of the process. In order to successfully leap it takes knowing that what we seek will be realized, along with trust in the intelligence that guides our experience every step of the way regardless of how it may appear on the surface.

Quantum physics asserts that none of our world is real or solid and that our consciousness is essentially hallucinating this experience of the physical, just as it does in the dreamscape; making it even more plausible that life is just a dream within the collective dream and the sooner we realize this the sooner we can become a lucid creator in the field of experience we encounter as our world.

Cerebral Clouds

If the physical world is as quantum physics asserts, an illusion, the solidity of which is essentially hallucinated by our perceptive functions, then all that actually exists of us is an energetic cloud full of neural lightning. Now from this perspective we can start to understand how limited we are by our conception of the physical and how infinite the possibilities are of the things we can experience as a cerebral energy cloud dreaming they are having this human experience.

If we take all of the physicality out of our conception of life on Earth what is left is an immense collective energy cloud formed entirely by a mass of individual cerebral clouds. The collective cloud is dreaming the experience of life on Earth and within this dream the individual is dreaming of their life on Earth. It is an incredibly cohesive and dynamic system, meaning both the collective affects the individual and the individuals affect the collective.

Every thought and feeling pulsates through the cloud of collective human experience transforming and evolving it and the same is true for the individual; every thought, feeling and experience is a new ingredient in the quantum soup that is our unique brand of energy. When we remove the illusion of the physical world simplicity begins to reveal itself. This perspective of the ephemeral mechanisms at play behind our experience of life really help to open us up to the possibilities. If this is really just a dream within a dream, then as we become aware of this we can begin to guide our personal dream and quite possibly the dream the collective is having as well.

Virtual Life

When I speak of the Game of Life what I'm referring to is the holographic field of experience we enter to learn, grow and explore. Imagine you are standing alone in the center of an empty room wearing virtual reality goggles, experiencing this life you are having right now. Imagine lifting the goggles up and seeing the empty space of the VR room, then placing them back on returning to the current setting you are surrounded by right now. Looking at life in this manner helps us to objectively understand its mechanics regardless of whether believe life to be a virtual experience program or not, this perspective helps reveal the way reality is built to operate.

There are no handheld controls to navigate this virtual reality of ours, it is designed to be infinitely responsive to our electromagnetic field which is the hybrid emanation of our thoughts and feelings. The only free will we actually have is the ability to consciously select our electromagnetic state, our frequency; the channel we are operating on. That in turn determines the bandwidth of experiences that are available to us to access at any given moment.

The Game of Life is finished, meaning the virtual program has been completed and contains an infinite number of possible experiences. This reveals to us the truth that we are not actually creating anything, merely calling it forth, much like the letters of the alphabet already exist and so too an infinite potential of combinations and expressions. The program has been designed with all possibilities, all versions and experiences we can fathom and each of them exists on a very specific electromagnetic frequency channel. The only way to access a specific experience in the program's library is to match the frequency bandwidth it exists within. Only then can and will it be realized. Now imagine watching this virtual reality we call our life and having no way to control or guide it, it feels like it's just happening to us but with experience we come to realize that the program is designed to respond to our mental and emotional states. That in fact our mental and emotional states are the only reality we actually experience, they are the lens, the goggles through which we experience and navigate the program which forms our reality.

Everything that we desire to be or experience already exists within the program library. We convince ourselves of the logical progression; all of the doing that needs to happen in order for us to believe it's possible to realize our desire. But if we are in fact just experiencing a virtual reality the act of doing is really quite irrelevant, it's just clips we are watching to build a story our mind finds believable by assembling a logical progression. But it's nothing more than a surface illusion, virtual clips pieced together through logic and resonance.

The only free will we actually have in this virtual program of life is to select our frequency, that is what allows us refine our energetic signature and call forth an experience from the program library; by connecting with its frequency bandwidth so we can be a resonant match. The only functional use that doing has is that it helps to get us to a specific frequency of operating at, which is what actually connects us to the experience we desire, not the doing itself. The only use doing has is that if done successfully the doing connects us with the state of being which in turn connects us with a desired experience within the virtual library.

Once we truly understand this process, we release the tethers of linear unfoldment and open up to a more multi-dimensional console system of experience. The linear logical means of doing greatly limits the results we can receive because it's time consuming and requires tedious incremental progression.

Anything you are doing is a surface illusion. What your thoughts and actions are really doing is transforming and anchoring the frequency you are operating on which in turn determines the bandwidth of experiences you can access.

This is the way the virtual life we are experiencing operates and once we fully integrate this understanding life becomes an immersive game of inner and outer exploration.

The universe favors the path of least resistance which means reality shifting and quantum jumping are really just a natural result of a profound shift in our frequency state. If we can definitively shift the baseline frequency of our electromagnetic field we can shift the reality we are experiencing instantaneously because life is just a virtual program of experience archives that are frequentially accessed, it's just that most people are greatly limited by the linear process of doing that we are indoctrinated with. If you can truly cultivate dominion over your electromagnetic state, you will be a master creator and by that I mean you will be a master accessor because in actuality we are not creating anything, just becoming adept at navigating the program's experience library.

The Masters

The Game of Life is essentially just a virtual holographic program that our cerebral-spiritual energy enters to evolve. The Ascended Masters are the ones who rose through all the levels and beat the game, and in doing so they helped to reveal the way for others. Just like us, these beings came into the experience program as virtual avatars and through rigorous ascension of the levels in both their inner and outer worlds they gathered the understanding of the way the program works and so they were able to claim their Creatorship and some even their Godship. Acts like resurrection, instant manifestation and spontaneous healings appear miraculous to those who do not yet understand how navigate the experiential field that makes up this virtual world we know as Life, but these things are available to every player who ascends the levels and masterfully refines their abilities.

These statements are not meant to sound irreverent or reduce the masterful acts of the ascended ones but rather to illustrate that we all contain the same power they do, most spent their entire lives trying to share that message with us.

The truly miraculous things every ascended master has achieved is their purity of heart, clarity of mind, and the indelible mark they have made on the world as they blazed a path they hoped we would all come to realize as well.

www.ingramcontent.com/pod-product-compliance
Lightning Source LLC
Chambersburg PA
CBHW070553170426